D1567414

The Perfect Square

The Perfect Square

A History of RITTENHOUSE SQUARE

Nancy M. Heinzen

TEMPLE UNIVERSITY PRESS PHILADELPHIA

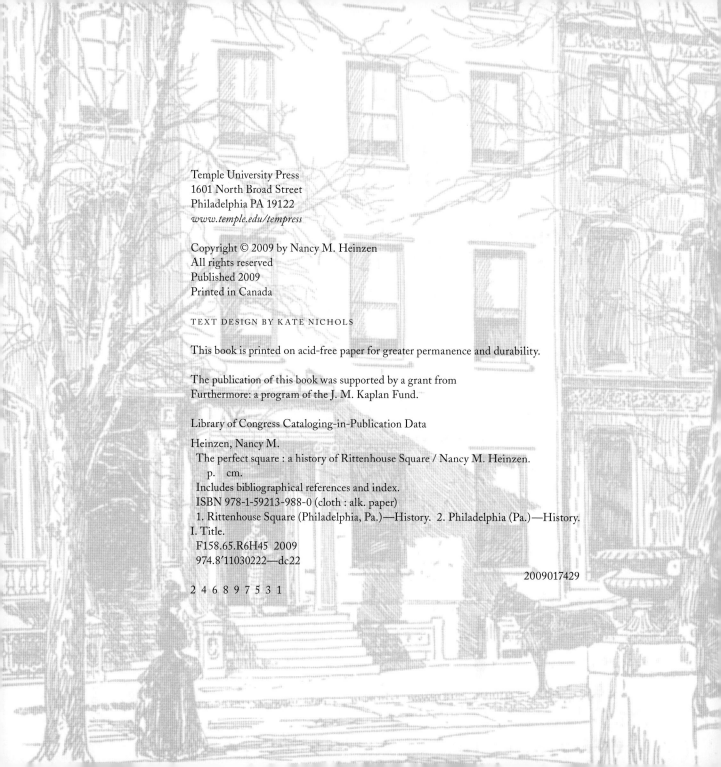

Temple University Press
1601 North Broad Street
Philadelphia PA 19122
www.temple.edu/tempress

TEXT DESIGN BY KATE NICHOLS

This book is printed on acid-free paper for greater permanence and durability.

The publication of this book was supported by a grant from
Furthermore: a program of the J. M. Kaplan Fund.

Library of Congress Cataloging-in-Publication Data

Heinzen, Nancy M.
  The perfect square : a history of Rittenhouse Square / Nancy M. Heinzen.
      p.   cm.
  Includes bibliographical references and index.
  ISBN 978-1-59213-988-0 (cloth : alk. paper)
  1. Rittenhouse Square (Philadelphia, Pa.)—History. 2. Philadelphia (Pa.)—History.
I. Title.
  F158.65.R6H45 2009
  974.8′11030222—dc22
                                                              2009017429

2 4 6 8 9 7 5 3 1

To Ben,

for his love, patience, and encouragement

[I saw] the residential square that lay before me shine in its native light. . . . I had only to turn round again and see where I was, and how it was . . . it having been clear to me still . . . that she couldn't *not* be perfect.

—HENRY JAMES, *THE AMERICAN SCENE*

Contents

Acknowledgments

THIS BOOK BEGAN as a collaboration with Jonne Smith, a neighbor who shares my enthusiasm for Rittenhouse Square. Although she subsequently withdrew from the project, Jonne graciously permitted me to make use of the ideas, research, and writing that she contributed during the years we worked together, many of which are woven into the tapestry of this book. Her knowledge and industrious participation added an important dimension to this book; indeed, without her involvement, the book might never have been launched. For all her valuable contributions to this work, I am deeply grateful. The book is a tribute to her generosity in seeing this work completed.

Dan Rottenberg, who has published many books and articles on Philadelphia history, was my editor and mentor in shaping the manuscript into the present text. I am indebted to him for his expertise, and especially for his good humor and moral support.

I am grateful to Micah Kleit, my editor at Temple University Press, for believing that Rittenhouse Square was a subject worthy of historic research. I thank

Emily Taber and Gary Kramer at Temple University Press for helping me to acquire the many permissions required for publishing the photos and illustrations.

I am similarly indebted to several curators and archivists, including Dana Lamparello at the Historical Society of Pennsylvania, Karen Lightner and Ted Cavanaugh in the Print Department of the Free Library of Philadelphia, Sarah Weatherwax and Nicole Joniec at the Library Company of Philadelphia, Holly Frisbee at the Philadelphia Museum of Art, Bill Whitaker at the University of Pennsylvania Architectural Archives, Dennis Buttleman of the Masonic Archives, John Pettit at the Temple University Urban Archives, Bruce Lavery, curator of architecture at the Philadelphia Athenaeum, and Susanna Thurlow of the Curtis Institute of Music.

I am also grateful to the Reverend Terrance Roper and Mary Louise Fleisher of the Church of the Holy Trinity, Deacon Bill Mays of St. Patrick's Church, and Brian McCloskey of Saint George's United Methodist Church.

In addition, I thank Rita Oaks for her graphic works, Karen Beck for her skills in bringing this book to its final stages, and Nancy Lombardi for her editorial expertise.

ACKNOWLEDGMENTS

XII

Prologue: Urban Oasis

[2000]

ON A PERFECT weekday evening in July, my husband and I sit in an outdoor dining alcove at a steakhouse in the Rittenhouse Hotel. The waning sun throws long slants of golden light into the treetops and along the facades facing west. Across the street on the west edge of Rittenhouse Square, couples stroll along the broad sidewalk, the better to see and be seen. Other strollers, their backs to us, lean against the iron fence surrounding the Square.

Inside the Square itself, families and groups of friends spread picnic blankets. The earliest arrivals sit on folding chairs in front of a portable outdoor stage. They are young, old, black, white, Latino, Asian. Some push baby strollers; others lean on walkers and canes.

All of us await a concert to be presented by students from the Academy of Vocal Arts, located just two blocks away. It is all part of Philadelphia's Welcome America Festival, held annually in recent years during Fourth of July week. This music, as much as our dinner, is what has drawn us to this alcove on the Square.

Within a few minutes the orchestra tunes up, and the young singers' voices float across the Square and beyond, rising above the noises of the crowd and the city. My husband and I wonder who the soprano is and try to guess what she is singing. A diner at the next table, overhearing us, offers us a program. He and his wife, he explains, are tourists from Santa Barbara, California. They spent the day visiting the ships and museums along Penn's Landing before meandering westward across Philadelphia's downtown Center City district. They happened upon this concert and this restaurant entirely by chance.

"What is this place?" they ask. We point out that the walk they have just taken replicates Philadelphia's westward expansion from the Delaware River waterfront in 1682 to this area in the 1850s. In a matter of two hours they have traversed nearly two centuries' worth of human endeavor, and the haven where they sit now represents the efforts of still another century and a half.

Of course, these tourists from California could make a similar journey in many other cities as well, but this gentle oasis in the heart of a bustling city is not so easily replicated. The passage of time alone cannot explain its creation or its survival. This place is unique, and so is the combination of human events and relationships that created and sustained it.

Governor's Woods

[1681–1825]

LIKE PHILADELPHIA ITSELF, the place known today as Rittenhouse Square existed in one man's imagination long before the first white settlers arrived.

William Penn saw little prospect that Quakers would be able to practice their religion freely in Restoration England. In this discouraged state of mind, in 1681 he prevailed upon King Charles II to pay off a debt to his father's estate by granting Penn a vast colony on the west bank of the Delaware River, across from the Crown colony of West Jersey, which had already been settled for some time. Penn conceived of this "Pennsylvania" as a refuge for all those persecuted for their beliefs, a beacon of religious tolerance, a peaceful oasis of brotherly love—in short, a community unlike any other in the Western world.

In a letter to a friend, Penn expressed the idea that his holy experiment was more suited to the New World than to England.

In July 1681, Penn announced from his home in England that he would establish a large town on the Delaware River. Philadelphia, as Penn named it, would be the modern world's first planned community. It would also be the world's only large city founded and profoundly influenced by Quakers.

As a young man in London, Penn had witnessed the bubonic plague of 1665 and the disastrous fire of 1666 that destroyed great areas of that densely populated city. So according to his plan, every house in Philadelphia was to be placed "in the middle of its platt [that is, its plot] . . . so there may be ground on each side for Gardens or Orchards or fields, that it may be a greene Country Towne, which will never be burnt, and alwayes be wholsome."[1]

Penn's so-called holy experiment was actually an odd combination of selfless communal ideals and materialistic land speculation. Penn was determined to demonstrate that idealism and commercial gain need not be mutually exclusive. "Though I desire to extend religious freedom," Penn wrote that same July, "yet I want some recompense for my troubles."[2] Planning a city in advance, he presumed, would provide some reassurance to potential investors who would otherwise feel skittish about buying land sight unseen.

But Penn himself did not arrive in Philadelphia until October 1682, and legal problems in England forced him to return there just two years later. So the challenge of translating Penn's utopian vision into reality on the banks of the Delaware fell to others: first the three commissioners he dispatched in the fall of 1681 to clear land and supervise the settlement; then the first settlers and landowners; and ultimately the millions of people who, during more than three centuries, chose to live and work in Philadelphia for diverse reasons that William Penn never anticipated. In retrospect, the remarkable thing about Philadelphia today is not how much the modern city has deviated from Penn's original vision in the course of those centuries, but how much of that vision has survived.

The boundaries of Penn's original rectangular city stretched some two miles from the Delaware River on the east to the Schuylkill River on the west, and from Vine Street on the north to Cedar Street (now South Street) on the south. Penn had presumed that his largest land purchasers would buy the desirable city lots along the shore of either river, or on the major thoroughfares, or around his five proposed squares, thus creating his imagined community. Yet almost from the first arrival, the settlers refused to behave according to Penn's plan, instead staking claims to country land beyond his plan and avoiding Penn's town altogether. (Penn himself would choose a tract of land on the northern border in "Liberty Land," far north of Philadelphia.)[3]

In 1683, to convince London investors of Philadelphia's viability, Penn's deputy governor, Thomas Holme, drew an elegant plan for Penn to use in London as a promotional tool, complete with a pitch written by Penn. Although the terrain between the two great rivers then consisted mostly of forests and hills, Holme mapped out the area like a checkerboard grid, as if a real city already existed there (Figure 1.1).

The centerpiece of Holme's map was a central "Square of ten Acres." Penn wanted this square to be surrounded by a Quaker meetinghouse, a school, and a market. In addition to the central square, four smaller squares, each of eight acres, anchored each of the city's four quadrants, each square named accordingly: Northeast, Southeast, Northwest, and Southwest.[4] In Penn's vision, these squares —which preceded any other plans for the city's design—"were to be as like the Moorfields in London." However, London's Moorfields were large, open, and unrestricted spaces; Penn's use of the word *square,* and the smaller space allotted to them, suggested that he more likely had in mind the smaller residential parks that existed in seventeenth-century London and Dublin, two cities with which Penn was familiar.[5]

Penn intended these four squares to remain open and accessible to all citizens forever, so he conveyed the title for the squares to the Commonwealth of Pennsylvania. Penn retained at least one side of each of the four quadrant squares for himself or his family, expecting to be able to resell these desirable locations at a nice profit once the area was developed. (On Southwest Square—later Rittenhouse Square—he kept the south side.)[6]

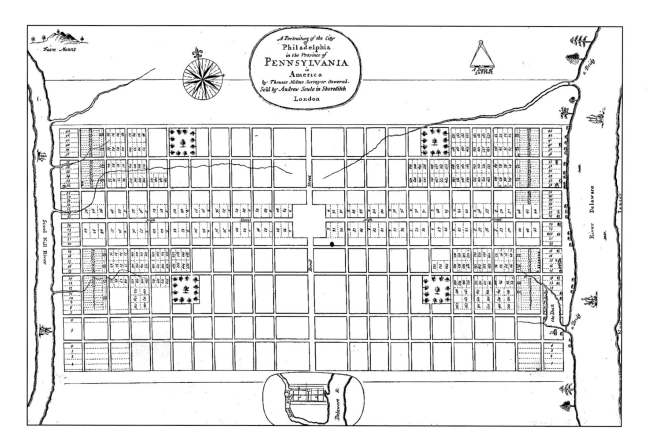

The plan for Southwest Square—the future Rittenhouse Square—called for forty-foot-wide streets on only two sides (the present-day Eighteenth Street and Walnut Street), to prevent roundabout horse traffic and to ensure quiet. Plots around the squares were made irregular in order to encourage the development of buildings with varied facades and multiple uses.

A list of first purchasers records lots on the northwest corner of Southwest Square (that is, the present corner of Walnut and Nineteenth streets) purchased by men named John Oldman, Robert Frame, Henry Bernard, and Richard Richardson. Who these men were and whether they actually took possession of their land is unknown. They were probably Quaker investors in England or Ireland who never immigrated to America. Because Penn knew that some buyers had made their land purchases as investments and had no intention of emigrating, he placed some of their lots along the Schuylkill River at the city's west end. This ploy created the impression that the city was widely settled along both rivers, when for all practical purposes these Schuylkill River lots lay deep within unsurveyed forest.[7]

Only one-third or fewer of Penn's original land purchasers in Ireland and England ever actually claimed their land in the western end. Indeed, for nearly a century most of Deputy Governor Holme's plan existed only on paper. As a city initially dependent on maritime trade, Philadelphia developed first along the Delaware River, where most commercial activity took place well into the nineteenth century. By the time Penn died in 1718, Philadelphia's Delaware River waterfront had become the most important port in Britain's American colonies, containing "above two thousand Houses, all Inhabited; and most of them Stately, and of Brick, generally three Stories high, after the Mode in London," in the words of one of the first arrivals.[8] Yet the area designated as Southwest Square lay deep in a forest known as the Governor's Woods, so called because most of the surrounding area was the Penn family's private property—an area that was effectively protected from early development and so remained the domain of hunters, fishermen, and picnickers for almost a hundred years.

A shipwrecked English trader named Richard Castleman, during a four-month sojourn in Philadelphia in 1710, described this area as excellent for hunting pigeons, doves, partridges, foxes, and deer; there were even accounts of wolves. The area had barely changed thirty-eight years later when another visitor, the Swedish botanist Peter Kalm, reported finding "a complete shade of forest trees, cooling and refreshing the whole road to Schuylkill," abundant with holly, dogwood, poplar trees, and wild pigeons that "flew in the woods in numbers beyond conception, and I was assured that they were more plentiful than they had been for several years past."[9] In 1720 the city passed a five-shilling fine for shooting pigeons on the streets, in effect restricting hunting to the Governor's Woods and beyond. A generation later Benjamin Franklin himself spoke of walks and rides to picnics out on the Schuylkill River, and of barge trips down the Schuylkill to visit the plantation of the botanist John Bartram, his good friend.

What Kalm and Franklin did not find was any evidence of the town that existed in William Penn's original sales plan: Walnut, Spruce, and Pine streets, Kalm wrote, "could not be traced by eye beyond Broad Street and even that was known but upon paper draft" (Figure 1.2).[10]

■ FIGURE I.2 *Schuylkill River, a bucolic scene prior to 1825. There were taverns and picnic areas along its banks from Fairmount to Grays Ferry.*

Kalm noted that the Governor's Woods remained a forest as long as it did only because the land was owned by absentee landlords, that is, people of means who did not consider the income that might be gained from the land, among whom were the Penn family. Ironically, precisely because Philadelphia initially failed to develop westward as Penn had intended, the area that became Rittenhouse Square was preserved in its natural state and eventually fulfilled Penn's original intent—the only one of Penn's four proposed squares to remain true to its original purpose, uncompromised (as the others have been) by use as cemeteries or (in the case of Northwest Square) the site of the public gallows.[11]

In 1741, Thomas Penn—the provincial governor since his father's death in 1718—sold parts of Northeast Square (now Franklin) and Southeast Square (now Washington) for burial grounds. The city attempted to recover those lands in 1800, and in 1836 the Pennsylvania Supreme Court voided Thomas Penn's sale as an "invasion of the permanent rights of the public square given by the founder in 1683."[12] It was the first of many instances in which either the law or private citizens protected the coveted lands of the original public squares.

Tradition has it that in 1777, shortly before the British army occupied Philadelphia, all the remaining trees west of the city to the Schuylkill River were chopped down and sold to Washington's Revolutionary army. An alternate version of this tale holds that the trees were cut before the British occupation to preserve firewood for citizens and prevent it from falling into the approaching enemy's hands. As loyal subjects of the Crown, the Penn family and other absentee landowners were now regarded as traitors, a perception that may have encouraged woodcutting on their land. In any case, with the coming of the Revolution the forest was gone, and the area west to the Schuylkill was now open land.

After the Revolution, with the Divesting Act of 1778, the Commonwealth of Pennsylvania—now a state of the United States of America—seized some twenty-two million acres from Tory loyalists, the Penn family among them. (Thanks to a City Council act designed to assuage the consciences of Pennsylvanians, the Penn family did ultimately receive some payment for its thirty thousand acres.) Among the appropriated properties were the five city squares. The Commonwealth held this land on the same terms as had the Penn family: The squares could not be sold or used for private benefit. The new terms authorized the Commonwealth to "make such regulations as to their convenience and adornment as shall best serve the purpose of health and recreation for which they were originally intended."[13]

By the time of the U.S. Constitutional Convention of 1787, pleasure gardens had sprung up along the Schuylkill River. Delegates to the Constitutional Convention that summer escaped the heat of the town by taking carriages out to Grays Ferry, there to enjoy the cooler breezes and the good food, music, and dancing provided by tavern keepers.[14]

A visiting New York businessman named Manassah Cutler remarked that summer that Pine Street was "no longer a shaded country walk, but a cobblestoned street, toward the Schuylkill River."[15] When his westbound carriage crossed Broad Street on its way to the amusement garden on the Schuylkill, Cutler's host drove him through what by then had become a "commons" of open fields where cattle and horses grazed. The area designated as Southwest Square was used to accommodate livestock and was still barely distinguishable from its surroundings. One hundred years after it was first marked on a map, Southwest Square was far from what Penn had envisioned, and far from what it would become. But the demands of an increasingly urban environment were about to change the Square.

PHILADELPHIA WAS ALREADY America's largest city when the U.S. Census of 1800 reported its population as 67,787. Penn's "greene Country Towne" was beginning to evolve into the first major American industrial city.[16] Although zoning was then unknown, social pressures served much the same function, pushing industries that were noisy, dirty, or smelly from the densely packed Delaware River waterfront into the western part of the city, where land was cheap and there were few influential neighbors to object. Manufacturers of pottery, porcelain, glass, white lead, and chemicals were scattered west of Broad Street. But the major businesses there were those related to construction, such as lumberyards, marble works, and especially brickyards.

Philadelphia lies on a bed of tough, high-grade clay—the primary material for bricks—all of it located within twelve feet of the surface.[17] When William Penn arrived in 1682, he found "Divers Brickerys" already functioning there. Brick houses had begun rising along the Delaware River, giving the city the look that would earn it the nickname "Red City." Brick making required little investment because the raw materials were everywhere; once the clay in a given yard was exhausted, a brickyard could simply move its wheelbarrows to another location and set up a new kiln there. As one observer remarked, in Philadelphia "a man could build a house of clay dug out of his own cellar."[18] But the process of weathering all this plentiful clay and baking it into bricks was dirty, labor-intensive, and brutally hot in the summer months, when the bricks were baked.

Brick makers went where they were needed to dig clay and form bricks near the new industrial construction expanding west toward Broad Street. (A 1777 map of Philadelphia shows six brickyards within two blocks of Southwest Square.) In Philadelphia's southwest quadrant, these clay excavations produced a landscape scarred by craters.[19]

After the land auctions following the Divesting Act of 1778, the lots on all four sides of Southwest Square passed into the hands of local owners, now American citizens. Among the other major purchasers of land west of Broad Street—William Binghams, Charles Biddle, Nicholas Easling, and Alexander Miller—none lived in the area; instead, they rented the land out to small merchants and brickyard owners.[20] Like William Penn's first purchasers, these men were land speculators, but this time their investments were ripe for development.

Typical of this new breed of owners was John Dunlap, who had come to Philadelphia from Northern Ireland as a child, part of a wave of Scotch-Irish immigrants, and eventually earned himself a footnote in history as the printer of both the Declaration of Independence and the Constitution.[21] Dunlap was a founder of Philadelphia's legendary First City Troop and fought with it during the Revolution. In the Commonwealth land auctions of 1783, Dunlap bought up many properties, but his motives were probably patriotic as well as commercial, since the proceeds from these land sales would be used to support the Continental Army. But Dunlap never intended to leave his home near his print shop in the old part of the city. His newly acquired land on the south side of Southwest Square was soon rented out for use as a brickyard.

Such enterprises, of course, were hardly the sort of use William Penn had originally envisioned. Penn, and most Philadelphians after him, had presumed that the guaranteed presence of the squares would naturally stimulate residential communities—not brickyards—around them. Yet, by the late eighteenth century, only the Northeast and Southeast squares (now Franklin and Washington, respectively) were actually viable urban spaces surrounded by structures.

The first evidence of citizen concern about the squares surfaced in the weekly *Pennsylvania Gazette* of February 29, 1792. "Purchasers next to these squares," the anonymous writer declared, "have paid more for their grounds in expectation of the original design being executed." Although Penn had never envisioned landscaping on the squares, the anonymous *Gazette* writer complained that the city had not improved the squares. Northeast (later Franklin) Square, "which lies at the entrance of the city by one of the most public avenues from the country, is become the receptacle of stagnant waters, of dung, human excrement, and all kinds of filth—so that a stranger passing into the city, instead of being saluted with beautiful appearances of groves, meets what is offensive to his eye and most of his other senses."

Planting trees in the squares, the *Gazette* writer claimed, "would conduce to the health of the city by the increased salubrity of the air, for it is an established fact, that trees and vegetation have a happy effect." The writer asked the city to "make provision for abating encroachments, removing nuisances, and improving and planting these squares with trees—the expence will be trifling." These same complaints and requests became a mantra for all of Philadelphia's squares over the ensuing generations.

As Philadelphia's brickyards and other industries moved west of Broad Street, unskilled and semiskilled laborers moved there as well to live close to their jobs. All across the area, the original large plots that William Penn had dreamed of were being broken up by side streets, alleys, houses, and courtyards, contrary to Penn's plan. By 1816, when John Dunlap sold his property on the south side of Southwest Square, this lot that had formerly been a brickyard now had houses on it. Ann Street (the present Manning Street) now bisected the block from east to west, just south of the Square; in the absence of another east-west street to the north, Ann Street became the de facto southern boundary of Southwest Square. Along this street lived an upholsterer, lumber merchant, and carpenter. A community was developing around the Square. And that year witnessed the first example of public financial support for what was to become Rittenhouse Square.

In April 1816, Philadelphia's City Councils—the city's legislature had two chambers at the time—passed a resolution to enclose the Square and to till and sod the parts overgrown with weeds and "not used for a particular purpose." (The "particular purpose" was probably a dump, as there is evidence that space on Rittenhouse Square was reserved for dumping through much of the nineteenth century.) The new fence prevented hogs, sheep, goats, and dogs from wandering into the Square. The need for a fence itself indicates that a residential population was growing around the Square—a population that wanted to separate the Square from the open pasturage, which was still in evidence on maps. (Local residents—probably property owners on the Square—provided the city with a four-year interest-free loan of $800 for the project.)[22] The resolution was an important step to prevent permanent encroachment.

In 1823 the former Dunlap property, which constituted the whole south front of the Square, was put up for auction. The city's official auctioneer, Tristram B.

Freeman, suggested in his newspaper advertisement that the property would be appropriate for "a place of worship, seminary, any public or private building." It added as a sales point: "Improvements are rapidly developing on Spruce Street."[23]

Two years later the Schuylkill canal opened, bringing anthracite coal—the cleanest and most efficient fuel yet known to humankind—to Philadelphia by barge from the coalfields of Schuylkill County. It was a watershed moment in the city's development: Access to coal would transform Philadelphia from a mercantile center dependent on oceangoing foreign trade to a self-sufficient industrial powerhouse known as "the workshop of the world" (Figure 1.3).

Soon the popular gardens and picnic spots and taverns along the Schuylkill from Fairmount to Grays Ferry were replaced by wharves that furnished new jobs heaving coal from the barges. This low-paying work went to poor, unskilled laborers who would soon swell the population close to the Schuylkill. In time the neighborhood developed a reputation as a rugged and dangerous area, dominated by street gangs like the "Schuylkill Wharf Rats" and the "Schuylkill Rangers."[24] Such people were hardly the genteel family patriarchs envisioned by William Penn, but they would in fact constitute the first residential community around Southwest Square.

IN 1825, FULLY 142 YEARS after Thomas Holme first drew them on his map, Penn's four original neighborhood squares—all but Center Square—were renamed in honor of prominent Americans (a departure from the Quaker precept against personal vanity). Precisely why the members of Philadelphia's two City Councils chose to name Southwest Square for David Rittenhouse is unknown: The Councils' minutes are vague on this point, other than to hint that they also considered naming it for Columbus.

David Rittenhouse, so far as we know, never saw or even knew of Southwest Square; his German Mennonite ancestors (originally called Rittenhausen) had first settled several miles north of Philadelphia in Germantown. But his mer-

its seem beyond dispute. David Rittenhouse had been one of Philadelphia's most accomplished citizens of the eighteenth century: statesman, patriot, first director of the U.S. Mint, president of the American Philosophical Society, and the most skilled clockmaker and builder of scientific instruments in colonial America. His orrery—a clocklike apparatus indicating the relative positions and motions of bodies in the solar system at any given time—was the scientific wonder of his age, and his published observation of the transit of Venus in 1769 earned him international recognition.

■ FIGURE 1.3 *The Schuylkill River after it was transformed by the Schuylkill Canal and the coal industry in 1825.*

Yet during his lifetime David Rittenhouse's remarkable achievements had been overshadowed by those of that superachieving Philadelphian, Benjamin Franklin; and Rittenhouse had died in 1796, just six years after Franklin. In the nearly thirty years since his death, Philadelphians had not come around to honoring David Rittenhouse. Now they had an opportunity to make amends: Southwest Square was renamed Rittenhouse Square.

Would this forlorn square in a marginal neighborhood reflect honor upon such an accomplished man? The answer to that question would be left to Philadelphians as yet unborn, most of whom would come in time to associate the name "Rittenhouse" not with any man, but with a location.

The Early Years

[1825–1844]

THE FIRST RESIDENTS around Rittenhouse Square in the late 1820s belonged not to the upper class but to the working class. Some of them made bricks in the nearby brickyards; others hauled coal from the barges on the Schuylkill; still others operated looms in their cellars or in nearby mills. Many were single immigrants from the British Isles who lived in boardinghouses; others were family men whose wives and daughters earned extra money working as weavers. For the most part their names cannot be found etched on marble monuments today. Yet their travails during the summer of 1832 sowed the first seeds of a dynamic urban community.

In 1832 the periphery of the Square was mostly open ground. On the south it was open to Ann Street (now Manning). On the east stood open low ground between Locust and Walnut streets. A few houses stood south of Locust along Eighteenth Street. On the north side of the Square stood two brickyards: one operated by the prominent politician (soon to be a U.S. congressman) James

Harper, and the other, just to the west, by a family named Lare, who also lived there. On the west side of the Square, between Walnut and Locust, stood still another brickyard. Between Locust and what is now Rittenhouse Square Street (not then in existence) was a clay pit pond.

Beyond the crude wooden fence along the south side of Rittenhouse Square that summer lay an open expanse of land down to Ann Street, where many of these working families lived in a dense jumble of tiny houses. A visitor who walks today along the 1800 block of this narrow alley may notice a row of small houses surviving from that period. These three-story row houses, now called 1830 Rittenhouse Court, housed family groups. In their courtyard they shared water pumps and privies, washed their clothes, and gossiped (Figure 2.1).

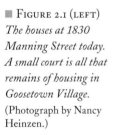

■ FIGURE 2.1 (LEFT)
The houses at 1830 Manning Street today. A small court is all that remains of housing in Goosetown Village.
(Photograph by Nancy Heinzen.)

■ FIGURE 2.2 (RIGHT)
The 1700 block of Manning Street today, with the homes of workers dating from the 1850s.
(Photograph by Nancy Heinzen.)

If we imagine other small houses like these—tightly clustered along courtyards, alleys, and walkways even narrower than Manning Street—we can envision the community that existed then. This was "Goosetown Village," so named because of the many geese drawn to the area by the numerous water-filled clay pits. With the benefit of an account written years later, we can reconstruct in our mind's eye a likely picture of this first Rittenhouse Square community as its residents went about their daily chores (Figure 2.2).

THE DATE IS July 19, 1832, proclaimed throughout Philadelphia as a "day of humiliation and prayer" for protection from the cholera epidemic. This plague had long been anticipated—with such fear that the port of Philadelphia had been quarantined during the previous winter. Nevertheless, the first cholera cases were reported in Canada that spring, and by June 1832 cholera had arrived in New York. By July 5, when the first case was reported in Philadelphia, most of the more privileged citizens who had not fled the city did so now.[1] But the poor residents of Ann Street had nowhere else to go. To these people, noted the diarist Joseph Sill, the issue of cholera was "the first remark to a friend or stranger after the customary salutation, and the last topic after every other subject has been exhausted" (Figure 2.3).

> When you rise in the morning, you are eager to get the last news respecting it [cholera] from New York; at noon-day you are seen hurrying to the office of the Board of Health for information of its progress here and at night you retire to rest with the express'd hope of its being better tomorrow.[2]

A prayer meeting had been scheduled in the Square the evening of July 19.[3] Earlier that day, in the sweltering heat, the women of Ann Street had scrubbed their washing in tubs of boiling water set in their communal yards. Then they

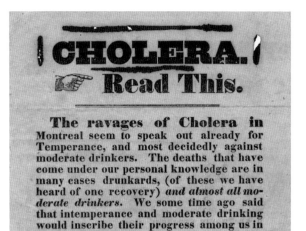

draped their household laundry over buttonbushes to dry in the hot sun.[4] By 3:00 P.M. the temperature stood at 88°F, the humidity was high, and dark clouds were rolling in on a gusty wind. With the first thunderclap of the coming storm, women burst out of the houses on the Ann Street courtyard, all running headlong toward the open lots to retrieve their clothes. But the downpour arrived too soon. The women—drenched along with their laundry—headed back home.

The women may have looked up briefly as they were joined by the brothers Peter and William Sipps, day laborers trudging home from the brickyards in mud-caked boots and shirts soaked with rain, after a day spent digging clay or carrying and stacking molded bricks. The coal heavers from the Schuylkill barges were returning home, too. It was a welcome reprieve from labor begun before daylight on that sultry day.

In dimly lit three-room houses, residents waited out the storm. They dried themselves and put on fresh clothes, then gathered around family supper tables. Then the residents of Ann Street began to spill out of their airless houses, which were much too small to contain for long their many occupants on this summer evening. Determined housewives carted their laundry back to the open lots on the south side of the Square.

Peter and William Sipps, freshly scrubbed and dry in their somber Sunday clothes, emerged from their home and strode toward the Square. Tonight they were returning to the brickyards, this time not to haul bricks but to assist Methodist ministers at a prayer meeting. They were "exhorters"—lay ministers who would beg the Almighty for deliverance from the cholera epidemic.

The Methodist prayer meetings were quite sensational, characterized by a fiery oratory style. Billy Barnes, a Philadelphia Methodist preacher of the day, was described by one observer as "wild in both his expressions and manner, so much so as to appear almost deranged."[5] Adam Wallace, a traveling Methodist preacher, described one of his congregants as a "shouter" who, joined by others, could bring "the most hardened sinners under conviction by their demonstrative exuberance."[6]

The Methodists had tried before to establish a church near Rittenhouse Square without success. But the absence of scientific explanations for the cholera epidemic gave religious leaders a fresh opening. To many ministers, cholera was a punishment for "ungodly practices." On the "day of humiliation and prayer," when the Methodists sent itinerant preachers "among the kilns and drying shelters of the brickyards" of Goosetown Village, the terrified residents of Ann Street were willing to listen.[7] The terrible scourge of cholera would prove instrumental in bringing the first church to Rittenhouse Square—and, with it, the first sense of community.

As the Sipps brothers walked toward the Square to participate in the Methodist meeting among the brick kilns, many neighbors joined them. Meanwhile, from the north side, a plane maker named Martin Summers also started toward the Square. Like most craftsmen, Summers maintained his shop in his home on George Street (now Sansom), a three-story house on a large lot where he lived with his wife. Like the Sipps brothers, Summers was a lay preacher. He was joined on his walk by the brothers John and Henry Lare, members of an extended family of brick makers who lived in two-story frame houses on narrow lots along what is now the 1900 block of Walnut Street. Because brick making was a seasonal job, the Lares also cultivated a field along Walnut Street, where they raised cabbages that they preserved as sauerkraut to sustain them through the winter when the brickyards shut down.[8]

Once the ordained preachers had delivered their open-air sermons in the Square that evening, the audience moved into the brickyard shelters where bricks were dried after baking. Here the Sippses and Summers took over, expanding the sermon to urge their penitent neighbors to confess and be saved. The voice of Martin Summers rang out "on the night wind in tones of agonized petition," according to one account.[9] From the little houses on Ann Street, those who stayed home could hear "cries of ecstasy" mingled with the voice of Summers.[10]

The powerful voices of the Sipps brothers probably carried across the Square. It may have reached the house on Ann Street where William Blanford lived with his wife, Rebecca, and their four children. Blanford was a civil servant—specifically, a watchman whose duty, in those days before urban police forces, was to walk the rounds, cry the hours, and "secure the peace and quiet of the city."[11] The Blanfords could have looked out from behind their house across open lots and onto the ponds, open sheds, and beehive kilns to the west of the Square, which glowed all through the summer nights. In the red glow of the setting sun that night, the Blanfords saw columns of smoke trailing across the open landscape and up into the sultry sky.[12] It was a "fitful, weird and thrilling" atmosphere, according to one observer (Figure 2.4).[13]

That night's prayer meeting seemed so uplifting that more such meetings were held through the summer. Over the next months clusters of Ann Street residents stood along the Square's fence in the evening, or people listened to the prayer meetings through open windows.[14]

Whether the meetings achieved their ostensible purpose—a reprieve from cholera—is a matter of debate: Eventually 779 of the 1,972 Philadelphians who

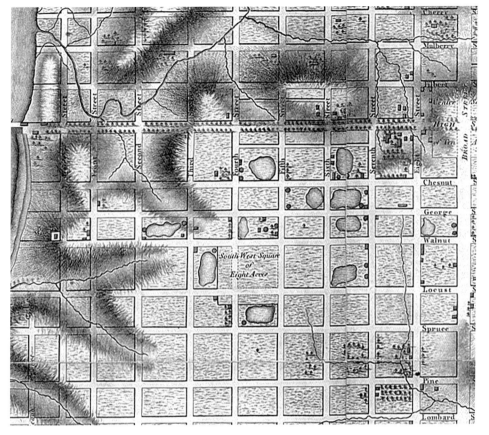

had contracted cholera died of it.[15] On tiny Ann Street alone, four residents died of cholera that August.[16] Yet by the end of summer the crisis had passed. "Many of the citizens who have been in the Country are now returning again, & the city begins to wear a more bustling appearance," Joseph Sill noted in his diary on August 27.

Yet that summer's prayer meetings produced a more lasting by-product. The Sipps brothers, Martin Summers, the Lares, and the Blanfords soon organized the area's first church, which was also the area's first communal institution.

The Western Methodist Church—most often called the Brickmakers' Church, for the brick makers who organized it—was the first of three churches established around the Square over the next twenty-five years, all within the same block. It was first envisioned in 1833, when a patent medicine purveyor named William Swaim donated property for a church on the east side of Twentieth Street near Walnut, not far from property he owned on the north side of Walnut.

Swaim himself did not live in the neighborhood, and his donation was probably motivated less by religious concerns than by (as a nineteenth-century Philadelphia Methodist history put it) "a view doubtless to the improvement of the neighborhood."[17] The lot Swaim contributed adjoined a clay pit pond next to the Square without an intervening street; so when the Brickmakers' Church opened there later that year, the west side of the Square was open all the way to Twentieth Street, and the rear of the new church was separated from the Square only by the Square's rough wood fence.

Because the congregants of the Brickmakers' Church were people of modest means, establishing it became a community project. Neighboring "boss brick makers" and lumberyard owners donated materials for the church. It is possible that one such boss was James Harper, who owned the brickyards at Nineteenth and Walnut and who would soon play a pioneering role in developing Rittenhouse Square as an upper-class neighborhood (Figure 2.5).

Harper's family had arrived in Philadelphia from Northern Ireland in 1791, when James was not yet ten. By the 1820s he had leveraged his success in operating a brickyard into a role as one of Philadelphia's leading citizens: He was a member of the Common Council, the Board of Prison Inspectors, and the board of the Guardians of the Poor. Harper was also a prominent Mason—he built Philadelphia's first Masonic hall—and presided when the Grand Lodge of Pennsylvania welcomed his fellow Mason, the Marquis de Lafayette, from France in 1824. Harper was elected to Congress in 1832.[18] Although Harper belonged to St. Stephen's Episcopal Church on Tenth Street below Market, his wife, Charlotte,

■ FIGURE 2.5
*A nineteenth-century
drawing of the process
of brick making.*
(Courtesy of Hagley
Museum and Library.)

attended Bible classes at the Brickmakers' Church all her life, and her name was inscribed in the church's records when she died in 1872.[19]

Another early pillar of the Brickmakers' Church—one who already lived on the south side of the Square—was a self-made linen weaver named William Divine, a Scotch-Irish immigrant whose father had run a textile mill in Belfast. Upon his arrival in 1827, Divine worked ten-hour days on a handloom, eventually working his way up to mill supervisor and then to owner of two other mills, one on Pine Street near Twentieth Street and the other on McDuffie Street (now Naudain) near what is now Twenty-first Street. By the 1830s, Divine and his wife, Margaret, had eight children. Although Divine's origins were working-class, in the process of making his fortune he became one of the first moneyed people living near the Square.

Also mentioned as "known to the members of the church" in its early years was Henry Wanamaker, a brick maker in Grays Ferry who, although not wealthy, may have contributed resources for constructing the Brickmakers Church. (Henry Wanamaker's son John, later the department store founder, organized a Sunday school at the Brickmakers' Church in 1858; and Henry's grandson Thomas would own a mansion on the Square later in the century.)

The Brickmakers' Church opened with two hundred members. Within the year the congregation was holding regularly scheduled Bible classes in the basement. Although a few members (like William Divine) eventually made their fortunes and moved into large houses on Rittenhouse Square, most church members remained weavers, coal heavers, brick makers, laborers, and craftsmen. The Lare children were baptized at Brickmakers' Church. Peter and William Sipps, laborers on weekdays, continued their lay ministries at the church. A boy known to posterity only as "AJR" wrote years later that he had learned to read in the basement of this church.

An 1839 guidebook noted that Philadelphia's western squares—Logan and Rittenhouse—were "not much used yet."[20] Yet urban development was beginning to move west past Broad Street. Beginning in 1833, horse-drawn omnibus service made hourly runs across the city along High Street (now Market). By 1836, Philadelphia's principal streets had been paved with cobblestones from the Delaware to the Schuylkill River and were lit by gas lamps. Formerly hilly streets were graded or built up to flatten the terrain to accommodate horse-drawn omnibuses[21]—no small task, since years of digging for bricks and clay on some lots had dropped the streets below their original level.[22]

By the 1850s, Philadelphia boasted some three hundred horse-drawn omnibus wagons, each colorfully decorated and providing service across town every fifteen minutes for as many as ten passengers sitting on narrow wooden benches.[23]

In 1834—the same year the Brickmakers' Church opened—the open land around Rittenhouse Square's periphery was replaced by a pair of streets, both fifty feet wide. West Rittenhouse Square Street and South Rittenhouse Square Street, as they were named, defined the Square's western and southern sides for the first time.[24] Consequently, the Brickmakers' Church and Ann Street could no longer consider themselves to be located "on the Square." On the other hand, these two new streets opened up the potential for real estate development along the Square's periphery.

Also about this time, Rittenhouse Square received its first landscaping. Carts of soil were brought in to level out the ponds and pits, saplings were planted, and graveled walks in a formal crisscross pattern showed up as early as 1838 on a survey map.

In 1840 the Philosophical Society proposed an astronomical observatory in the Square to honor the Square's scientist namesake, David Rittenhouse. The Square was well suited for an observatory, its advocates argued, because "it would allow of a sufficient horizon, and be at such a distance from the crowded streets as to be beyond the agitation consequent on the passage of carriages on the pavement."[25] The City Councils approved the proposal, but with the caveat that the observatory could be removed by the mayor or councils at any time; and consequently the Philosophical Society decided the observatory was a risky use of its money and withdrew its proposal.

This was the first time any government entity intervened in the life of Rittenhouse Square. The observatory also represented the first of many proposals for the Square—from playgrounds to parking garages—that were never consummated. In this case it was just as well that the proposal was withdrawn: The Philosophical Society lacked the foresight to predict the neighborhood's explosive growth. As the old city center moved westward, property values west of Broad Street doubled from 1829 to 1835 and then tripled between 1835 and 1841.[26] Within a few years, huge construction projects would obstruct the "sufficient horizon" needed for an observatory.

The growth of the community led to the creation of a second church in 1839. St. Patrick's ministered to newly arrived Irish Catholic immigrants in a largely Protestant community.[27]

The group's leader was Paul Reilly, a bailiff at the State House who lived nearby. At first the group rented a former vinegar factory on Nineteenth Street between Ann (later Manning) and Spruce and used it as a church and school.[28] But the growing numbers of Irish Catholics in Philadelphia needed more than a place to worship; they also needed protection from nativist prejudices. To meet these needs, Reilly and his fellow Catholics petitioned Bishop Francis P. Kendrick to purchase land in the area.

It was an inauspicious time to found a Catholic parish in America, for Catholic churches had become symbols of the "hated foreigners," whom some people blamed for snatching jobs from native-born Americans. Although Philadelphia was the country's greatest manufacturing city, like the rest of the country it needed more than a half dozen years to recover from the Panic of 1837, America's first major economic depression.

The Native American Party, sometimes called the Know-Nothings by their opponents, rose out of this unrest.[29] "The object of this party," the Philadelphian Sidney Fisher remarked in his diary, "is the exclusion of foreign-born from a share in the political power of the country."[30]

Mob violence, Fisher added, was "what we must now consider one of the usual & necessary evils of our execrable government."[31] James Harper found himself a target when he introduced a mechanical brick-molding device to increase production and minimize costs. His workers, fearing that this device might cause layoffs and thereby take "bread out of their children's mouths,"[32] turned to violent demonstrations to make their point.

The danger of arson aimed at a Catholic church was real. But instead of moving to an isolated location for their self-protection, the organizers of St. Patrick's parish adopted the opposite strategy. On July 4, 1841, they laid the cornerstone for the new St. Patrick's Church at the corner of Twentieth and Murray (now Rittenhouse Square Street), in the midst of a community of frame dwellings of Protestants and less than a block south of the Brickmakers' Church, also on Twentieth

Street near Walnut. Such close proximity, they astutely perceived, was the best way to protect the church from being burned.[33] When Paul Reilly was challenged on the wisdom of locating the new church in hostile Goosetown, he replied, "I see flames in the air, but these enemies will not risk their own properties."[34] If the church burned, so would the frame houses of non-Catholics surrounding it. Reilly counted on the self-interest of the community to overcome bigotry, and in this case his gamble succeeded.[35]

The amenities of a community—two churches, paved and graded streets, gaslights, and public transportation, as well as trees within Rittenhouse Square itself—were now in place. All that remained was for someone of means to recognize the neighborhood's potential as an enclave of elegance.

The first such gentleman was Philip Physick, son of the noted surgeon Philip Syng Physick, the celebrated "Father of American Surgery," who pioneered the use of autopsies and stomach pumps and counted President Andrew Jackson and Chief Justice John Marshall among his patients. His lawyer son appears to have been eager to distinguish himself from his celebrated father without quite knowing how.

A year after his father died in 1837, the younger Philip Physick used his inheritance to buy five contiguous lots at the northwest corner of Nineteenth and Walnut streets, far from his father's home on Fourth Street.[36] This property had changed hands many times since the Revolution and had been divided into smaller lots, all inhabited by working-class families, much like the rental properties on the south side of the Square. The red frame houses of the Lare clan with their cabbage patch stood adjacent to Physick's property. Harriet and Martin Summers and their children still lived at 1930 George Street (now Sansom). James Harper's brickyards stood to the east across Nineteenth Street.

Philip Physick proposed to reverse this pattern: He would consolidate all five properties and build himself a Greek Revival mansion designed by the prominent architect John Haviland.[37] "Physick's Folly,"[38] some people called it, with good reason: To build such an elaborate home in an undeveloped area, cheek by jowl with brick pits and cabbage beds as neighbors, was indeed a reckless act (Figure 2.6).

Physick's house, according to one description, had "a classic front, expansive dimensions and grandeur of style, including a large hall from which a circular stairway led to the third story, lighted by a rotunda lantern." The house was so large, with such a complex interior structure, that at least one neighbor child

recalled years later that he once "got lost in the numerous upper chambers, with communicating doors, mischievous companions having locked the doors of the exit to the stairway. My sister found me after an hour's hunt, and I never forgot that only hour of imprisonment."[39]

The house took four years to build, and its cost seriously exceeded the architect's estimates. By the time it was finished, Physick had lost much of his inheritance by investing it in a commercial scheme to raise silkworms. Unlike the self-made weaver William Divine—who made his fortune by betting his future on wool—Physick lost his fortune by betting on silk. When he proved unable to pay his creditors, his unfinished house was sold in a sheriff's sale in 1843, before he had spent one night there.[40] It remained unoccupied until 1848.

In retrospect, Physick was a visionary who was well ahead of his time. But his audacious (albeit unsuccessful) venture emboldened other gentlemen of his class to pursue similar experiments nearby.

Across the street from Physick's house, on the northeast corner of Nineteenth and Walnut streets, John Hare Powel constructed a villa on a large lot between 1839 and 1840. Like Physick, Powel came from a prominent Philadelphia family. His uncle, Samuel Powel, was a two-term mayor of Philadelphia in the eighteenth century, and John had served with distinction as a diplomat in London and as a colonel in the U.S. Army. Following his marriage in 1817, Powel and his bride had moved to an estate he called Powelton, west of the Schuylkill River, where John had devoted himself to experiments in agriculture and animal husbandry. He was fifty-three in 1839 when he built a second villa for himself on Rittenhouse Square, apparently more as an investment than as a residence: Like Physick, neither Powel nor his family seems to have spent much time living on the Square.

But the third such mansion represented a practical vision that finally took hold. In 1840, James Harper, the brickyard owner and former congressman, began building a home in the middle of the 1800 block of Walnut Street (Figure 2.7).[41]

■ FIGURE 2.7 *James Harper, brickyard owner on the north side of Walnut Street, between Eighteenth and Nineteenth streets. He was the Square's first real estate developer.*

Unlike the Square's absentee landowners of the previous generation, or the recent real estate dilettantes like Physick and Powel, Harper was already an established presence in the neighborhood. Since 1813 he had operated a brickyard along the north side of Walnut between what are now Eighteenth and Nineteenth streets. He had gradually acquired all the adjacent lots on Walnut Street. He hoped to generate income both by selling his lots and by selling the bricks for the houses that would be built on them. Unlike Physick and Powel, Harper was investing in a community that was already his own and where he planned to remain. He also reserved a lot next door to his own house for his married daughter Annie and her husband, George Peabody.

Harper's house was smaller and less impressive than "Physick's Folly." But like the Physick house, Harper's house contained white marble elements in a Greek revival style on its front portico. Although Harper's narrow lot was smaller than either Physick's or Powel's (twenty-eight feet wide, compared to a hundred feet for Physick's), it was large enough for a two-story coach house and a five-horse stable facing George Street (later Sansom) in the rear. Harper built his home in the narrower Philadelphia row house tradition, rather than the villa style of Physick or Powel, calculating that narrower lots along Walnut Street would increase the number of potential sales (Figure 2.8).

These new large homes rising on the Square in the early 1840s remained anomalies in a neighborhood more characterized by the narrow streets and modest wooden houses of Goosetown. James Harper the retired congressman still coexisted with the brick workers of the Lare family and their rustic vegetable patch next door. The neighborhood was epitomized neither by Harper nor Philip Physick nor John Hare Powel but by the night watchman William Blanford of

■ FIGURE 2.8 *James Harper's house, from a picture circa 1880.* (Print and Picture Collection, Free Library of Philadelphia.)

Ann Street, who sat every night in a gray wooden street corner watch box large enough to hold a stove and a seat, emerging each hour to cry, "Past two o'clock and a starlight morning."[42] But Blanford and his Goosetown neighbors and their quaint occupations—indeed, Goosetown itself—would soon become vestiges of the past. James Harper was the precursor of Rittenhouse Square's future.

Bricks and Mortar

[1844–1863]

IN THEIR FOUR-STORY mansion on Walnut Street, James Harper and his family could survey the city in all directions from any one of the six windows in the cupola.[1] So they were probably uniquely positioned on the nightmare evening of May 6, 1844, when the smoke of smoldering torches illuminated the shadowy forms of men on foot and on horseback, armed with brickbats, muskets, and pistols.

Some were weavers from William Divine's textile mills on McDuffie Street (later Naudain), and some were laborers from Harper's own brickyards. The volunteers also included dockworkers who lived in the small alleys and courts around St. Patrick's Church. All were gathering within Rittenhouse Square's white wooden fence to defend St. Patrick's Church against nativist mobs that roamed the city that night. Philadelphia's "Awful Riots of 1844" were under way, and the residents of Goosetown were fashioning their unique response.

Earlier that day, a Nativist Party rally at Second and Master in Kensington— outside the city but less than two miles from Rittenhouse Square—had erupted in violence between the nativists and the Irish Catholics who had gathered to protest the rally. The fighting broke out in a crowd estimated at four thousand people. Then the violence began to spread into neighboring communities, threatening Catholic churches and homes (Figure 3.1).[2]

St. Patrick's, the Catholic church built by Irish immigrants in the heart of Goosetown, was vulnerable. So was anyone—Catholic or Protestant—who lived nearby. James Harper was a Protestant (albeit with Irish roots), but his own considerable real estate investments near St. Patrick's were at risk. The concept of a citywide police force was unknown at the time: Local constables exercised lim-

■ FIGURE 3.1 *Anti-Catholic riots in 1844 began in Kensington and had repercussions that were felt in Rittenhouse Square.*
(The Historical Society of Pennsylvania [HSP], *Riot in Philadelphia* lithograph.)

ited authority restricted to their own neighborhood districts. Consequently, when word of the riots reached Goosetown, private citizens gathered to protect the church, even while city officials organized armed companies of citizen guards.[3]

The latter-day Paul Revere in this case was Dr. Thomas Stokes, a Catholic physician whose position as the city's health officer involved boarding ships from abroad as they entered Philadelphia's harbor and quarantining them if he found disease aboard. Like Paul Revere in 1775, Stokes now rode through the streets to warn the Rittenhouse Square neighbors of the mob feared to be moving across the city from Kensington. He alerted Paul Reilly, who, along with Stokes, had spearheaded the building of St. Patrick's Church five years earlier. Although St. Patrick's stood on Twentieth Street, at this time it actually fronted on Rittenhouse Square because no other buildings stood between the church and the Square. Now Stokes and Reilly rallied the congregation to defend their new church.

As Reilly had anticipated when the church was built, Protestants and Catholics alike rallied to protect the church in the midst of their community. Some Protestants recruited by Reilly—like Singleton Mercer, president of the Farmers and Mechanics Bank, and Joseph Swift, "gentleman"—were motivated by sincere altruistic concerns toward their Catholic brethren. Others may have been motivated more by their selfish concern that any fire at St. Patrick's could easily spread to the two-story frame houses that constituted most of Goosetown.[4]

Stokes organized an outpost of the unmarried men assembled on the Square to form a front line against any mob, probably on the theory that single men were more expendable because they had no families to support. Meanwhile, Reilly formed the married men in a protective circle around the church itself.[5]

Over the next five days, as the rioting continued, many businesses closed their doors. While the black smoke rose from fifty houses along the Delaware River going up in flames less than two miles to the east, a circle of men barricaded St. Patrick's Church. On Wednesday morning, May 8, St. Michael's Church at Old Kensington and North Girard streets burned. At 10:00 that night the ringing of the State House bell announced another alarm to the east: the glow of what the diarist Thomas Cope called "a powerful light. The flame ascends higher & the whole City is lighted up." St. Augustine Church near the Delaware River was burning, creating "an eerie atmosphere under the moonless canopy of clouds." At 11:30 the State House bell continued to ring, "reminding us," Cope noted, "of the awful tocsin of Revolutionary France. After 12 . . . the sky [is] still reddened with the embers of St. Augustine's Church."[6]

On Thursday, May 9, with the smell of smoke in the spring air, the state militia arrived, summoned by Governor James Patterson to protect Catholic property.[7] Although the city remained quiet, Sidney Fisher noted in his diary that "citizens [were] advised to arm. . . . Martial law was in effect proclaimed. Troops were stationed at all expected points of attack."[8] Wrote Cope, "The City presents the appearance of a garrisoned Town. We meet armed men everywhere. Several companies arrived from the country yesterday & it is said that we are now guarded by four thousand soldiers under arms."[9]

On Sunday, May 12, Catholic churches were closed, and armed troops guarded streets leading toward them. By the time peace was restored, forty people had died. Yet the violence never reached Rittenhouse Square. The men there who had put their lives on the line could at last return to their homes and families.

On the following Sunday, St. Patrick's Catholic Church opened its doors to the faithful once again (Figure 3.2). Thanks to the cooperative spirit of its nearby residents, Rittenhouse Square had been spared the trauma suffered by other parts of the city.

One by-product of this violent episode was a movement to consolidate Philadelphia with its surrounding county, the better to develop a unified and disciplined police force. In effect, consolidation would expand the city's jurisdiction beyond William Penn's original boundaries—Vine Street to South Street between the Delaware and Schuylkill rivers—to embrace such villages as Kensington, Spring Garden, Moyamensing, and Passyunk (then called "the Liberties"). When

■ FIGURE 3.2 *The first St. Patrick's Church, on south Twentieth Street, built in 1843.* (Photo courtesy of St. Patrick's Church.)

consolidation took effect in 1854, it opened up opportunities in police work that had not previously existed. William Blanford, Rittenhouse Square's familiar night watchman, would leave his job to become a policeman. His son John would follow in his father's footsteps and join the force as well.[10]

William Divine's textile mills remained intact to exploit the boom in military goods that would come with the Civil War in the 1860s. And James Harper's considerable real estate investment in the future of Rittenhouse Square was secure. In the 1850s, Harper would be able to sell off the Walnut Street lots he had accumulated over the previous thirty years. In the process of turning a profit for himself, he also helped determine the direction that development would take around Rittenhouse Square for the rest of the nineteenth century.

Perhaps the first sign of Harper's prescience was the arrival of the businessman and civic leader Henry Cohen, descended from a prominent Philadelphia

■ FIGURE 3.3 *Henry Cohen, a resident of 1828 Rittenhouse Square. He was an ardent promoter of the Union cause and an early member of the Union League.*

Jewish family (Figure 3.3). (His grandfather, a linguist and rabbi whose congregants included Philadelphia's famous Gratz family, had arrived in America from England in 1792, a year before the young James Harper.) The Cohen family lived on Chestnut Street near Broad until 1851, when a collision of coal cars on the freight rail tracks running down the middle of Broad Street had reverberated through the Cohens' house, causing the pantry shelves to collapse and destroying Mrs. Cohen's cherished sets of Copeland china. This domestic catastrophe had been the final straw for Matilda Cohen: The family had packed up and moved west to the more tranquil neighborhood on the south side of Rittenhouse Square, then the western edge of the developed city.[11]

The Cohens were soon followed to the Square's south side by Francis M. Drexel, an Austrian painter who had arrived in Philadelphia in 1817 and opened a currency brokerage on Third Street twenty years later. By the late 1840s, Drexel and his sons Francis A. and Anthony had the city's largest banking and brokerage business, but they were still perceived as outsiders in international banking circles and Philadelphia social circles alike. Such a family, just on the cusp of respectability, needed to pay closer attention to its image, and so in 1852 the patriarch Francis M. Drexel moved westward with his family to the south side of Rittenhouse Square at the corner of Nineteenth Street. His sons and their new wives lived there briefly as well.[12] Like James Harper before them, the Cohens and Drexels had both money and the sort of liberated psyches capable of envisioning new possibilities, and their presence on the Square attracted other like-minded residents.

IN 1853 THE SQUARE was enclosed by an iron fence on the four streets surrounding it, creating a psychological border for what had previously been an open park bordered only by a rough board fence. At the same time, three large ornamental fountains were installed inside the Square. At the entrance to the northwest corner, a fountain presided over by the god Mercury was donated by the civic leader J. Gillingham Fell. At the northeast corner, *Aquarius* was the gift of Moses Brown Ives Goddard, of Providence, Rhode Island. (The donor of the third ornamental fountain is unknown.)

Outside the Square's iron gate, on Walnut between Eighteenth and Nineteenth streets, two smaller public drinking fountains were placed, as well as a trough for horses. These fountains sought to serve a nationwide temperance movement by encouraging the drinking of water rather than whiskey. In any case, the combination of the impressive fence and the fancy ornamental fountains reinforced the Square's image as a special place (Figure 3.4).

But the grand fountains were not universally appreciated. Subsequent public opinion judged the fountains inside the Square as "tall, grotesque and fanciful," and they were eventually removed by the City Councils' orders—not for esthetic reasons, but because their overflow muddied men's trousers and women's skirts.[13]

The Square was illuminated at night with gas lamps, and benches were installed, replacing the old round-topped wooden stools. The grass, which had previously grown wild in the summer, was now "frequently cut and trimmed," according to a local guidebook.[14] The red gravel walks were well rolled and kept clean.[15]

The 1853 iron fence, six feet high, was a sign of the Square's transformation into an urban park appropriate to the toney mansions now springing up around it.[16] Swinging gates at the corners, which were locked at dusk, intersected this railing. The much-feared constable, Dandy Stokes, rang a warning bell to announce the closing. Anyone who was locked in would have to climb the high spiked fence "to the injury of one's clothing," as Charles Cohen remembered.[17]

FOUNTAIN—RITTENHOUSE SQUARE.

■ FIGURE 3.4 *The fountains on the left and at center, circa 1850, were ornamental and stood inside the Square. On the right is one of two fountains with a horse trough on one side and a drinking fountain on the opposite side. These were located at Nineteenth and Walnut streets and Eighteenth and Locust streets.*

From this period on, when people referred to "Rittenhouse Square," they meant not only the six-acre square itself but also the fine architecture around it. The term also referred to the Square's local inhabitants, now growing in numbers as well as prestige.

The area beyond the large houses on the periphery of the Square, however, was a different story. Vast open grazing lots still punctuated the homes and factories scattered from Broad Street to the Schuylkill River, and the rough nature of these neighborhoods inevitably impinged on the relatively sedate life of the Square. Into the 1880s, animals were driven during the night or early morning hours along Chestnut Street to slaughterhouses on the Schuylkill River. (About this time, several albino deer were given to the city and housed in Logan and Rittenhouse squares.)

IN 1855 A VAST CONSTRUCTION PROJECT began on the east side of the Square, encompassing the entire block from Locust to Walnut streets between Seventeenth and Eighteenth streets. Here in the westernmost residential area of the city, within sight and smell of mills, factories, and breweries, Joseph Harrison was building a mansion modeled after the Pavlovski Palace in St. Petersburg, with an attached gallery for his newly acquired art collection.[18]

Like James Harper and William Divine, Harrison was a self-made man, but on a much more spectacular scale. As a young apprentice, he designed a locomotive engine that impressed a visiting Russian trade delegation, which subsequently offered him a contract to build a railroad between Moscow and St. Petersburg. Although he had only $500 in his pocket when he went to Russia, he declined to charge a flat fee for his services, instead negotiating for a royalty to be paid for every individual transported over the railroad during a specific period of time. As circumstances would have it, the Crimean War broke out in March 1854, and Russian troop movements to the war zone over his rails ensured Harrison a huge fortune.[19] He returned to Philadelphia after a grand tour of Europe—where, with his new fortune, he amassed a fabled art collection. (It later became a centerpiece of the Pennsylvania Academy of the Fine Arts collection.)[20]

By 1855, Harrison was forty-five years old and one of America's wealthiest men, and consequently his proposed mansion project vastly eclipsed Harper's earlier structure (as well as the Physick and Powel houses) in grandeur as well as size. Its gallery wing held Harrison's extensive art collection, and the large marble swan in its second-story window became a neighborhood landmark.[21] In addition to his home, Harrison's project included a row of town houses along Locust Street, a communal garden, and a block of stables facing Chancellor Street (Figure 3.5).[22]

As this massive excavation project got under way, groups of curious onlookers gathered along the newly installed iron fence and drinking fountain on the east side of Rittenhouse Square to watch. Among the informal sidewalk superintendents was Henry Cohen's young son Charles, who lamented the loss of an open patch that he and his friends had used in

winter as a skating rink—one of the few ice fields, he later recalled, where "reputable people" could skate without fear of the rougher element.[23] "Our skating was at an end," Charles noted, and so were their soccer games. But the compensation was

> the boyish delight in watching the method of excavation accomplished by digging under a section of earth which was toppled over by the use of crowbars, creating a thundering noise to be heard at a great distance, the earth being subsequently removed in small horse-drawn carts, the only known method at that time. Up to that period there probably was no building of such a character erected in any other city of the United States.[24]

By the time Harrison's mansion rose on the east side of the Square, James Harper's thirty-year real estate investment on the north side had begun to pay off when he found buyers for his large lots along Walnut Street. It was at this time that Harper, by virtue of his service as a legislator and civic leader, changed his listing in the city directory from "brick maker" to "gentleman." In its basic original sense, the term *gentle man* meant someone who did not work with his hands, and consequently justified his existence by upholding standards of culture, manners, taste, and breeding. Harper's Walnut Street home was now surrounded by neighbors whose owners also called themselves gentlemen. By the 1850s, the south side of the Square too was completely developed along South Rittenhouse Square Street (where the Cohen family lived). In 1849, William Divine—by this time owner of several textile mills—had moved his wife, Margaret, their eight children, and five Irish domestics from their modest house on Spruce Street north to a more comfortable home at the corner of Eighteenth Street and South Rittenhouse Square.[25]

Like many of their neighbors, the Divines upheld the spirit of William Penn's "greene Country Towne" by maintaining a large garden along Eighteenth Street, where Charles Cohen recalled the Divines tending "fruit trees in abundance, with an arbor for grapes and wisteria, and in the center were two stones from the Giant's Causeway in Ireland."[26]

Their northward view across the Square on a May evening in 1851 was tranquil compared to the armed preparations that James Harper's family had witnessed from the north side just seven years earlier. "I called at the [Divine] house last night," wrote a visitor named Allen Candelet, "sat awhile with Mrs. Divine . . . and the children were all romping in the Square and could not find time to come to supper."[27]

Meanwhile, on the Square's west side, two major buildings sprang up where the brickyards (now abandoned) had operated barely a decade earlier. Fairman Rogers was just twenty-three years old in 1856 when he built a plain but substantial brick home at 202 South Nineteenth Street whose greatest attractions were its modern conveniences inside. Unlike Harper and Harrison, who earned their "gentleman" titles, Rogers inherited his status from an established Chester County family. He was a University of Pennsylvania graduate, a horseman, a collector of American art, and a founder of the Rittenhouse Club.[28]

But the greatest symbol of Rittenhouse Square's arrival as a bastion of Philadelphia's upper class was the construction, in 1857, of the neighborhood's great Episcopalian house of worship. The Church of the Holy Trinity would be the third church in the block between Nineteenth and Twentieth, Walnut and Rittenhouse Square streets. The existing St. Patrick's and Western Methodist catered to brick makers, weavers, laborers, and dockworkers, but Holy Trinity would minister to gentlemen, in the belief that, as one wag later put it, "Our Lord was a gentleman."[29]

Two years before construction of Holy Trinity began, a planning committee recognized the desirability of the Rittenhouse Square area as a residential community and prime location for a church. Several members of the committee were among the prominent Philadelphians building around the Square. They included

James Harper's son-in-law, George Peabody, and others who had purchased lots from Harper.[30]

They conceived their church as a counterpoint in architectural splendor to the Harrison mansion project across the Square, drawing its congregation from its increasingly prosperous neighbors. Indeed, many of the new residents, including Harrison, would join Holy Trinity's congregation. Both Holy Trinity and St. Mark's were Episcopal churches within three blocks of each other. Generally, St. Mark's was for the Catholics turned Episcopalian (like the Meades and Drexels), while Holy Trinity was for the Quakers turned Episcopalian (like the Lippincotts and Prices).[31]

The committee chose as its architect John Notman, who in 1848 had designed the neighborhood's first Episcopalian church: St. Mark's, three blocks east on Locust Street. Notman designed both churches according to the popular Victorian brownstone model. His original pretentious design for Holy Trinity called for 1,500 seats as well as a "Norman" steeple 225 feet high above the 84-foot tower— "taller than anything in town," as its pastor Phillips Brooks later disparagingly described it. (The plan for the spire was subsequently discarded, although apparently for practical rather than theological reasons.)[32]

When the neighbors heard in 1857 that their fishing pond on the west side of the Square would be drained to build Holy Trinity, the curious and idle reconvened to watch workmen dig a trench to drain the property. Once the draining began, the churning waters of the draining pond revealed a bounty of fish below the surface. At this moment the onlookers scattered in all directions, returning soon with shovels, buckets, and tubs. Crouching beside the trench, they scooped up loads of the catfish that choked the ditch.[33] That tumultuous scene represented the last hurrah of Rittenhouse Square as a working-class neighborhood. By May 26, 1857, the pond had been drained and filled in, and a very different group gathered to celebrate the placing of Holy Trinity's cornerstone (Figure 3.6).

■ FIGURE 3.6 *The Church of the Holy Trinity under construction, circa 1857. It was designed by John Notman in the Norman style; a 225-foot steeple included in the original design was never built.* (The Library Company of Philadelphia.)

For clergymen, like real estate developers, the first measure of success is the ability to attract a clientele. In that sense, Holy Trinity succeeded from its first service on March 27, 1859. Within two years every pew was rented or sold. The opening of Holy Trinity also launched a new fair-weather tradition: the after-church "Sunday stroll," in which congregants in their finery paraded along Walnut Street and through the Square, which now boasted walks within its high surrounding railing and fine houses on all four sides—a scene that the diarist Sidney George Fisher found "suggestive of Hyde Park in London" (Figure 3.7).[34]

As the neighborhood around Rittenhouse Square became more residential, for the first time in its history the Square took on the role of a neighborhood park. Every morning, neighbors greeted each other as they crossed the Square to businesses or errands. Through their front windows, mothers could monitor their children playing in the Square while the children enjoyed a sense of relative autonomy. The children found their fondest adventures, of course, beyond their mothers' view. "We boys used to gather at the Square after dark," recalled Frederick Shelton, a youthful companion of Charles Cohen in the 1850s,

and climb over the fence, when the constabulary was not looking, and roam around inside, chiefly, I take it now, because we were doing something that we were not supposed to do. We used to spot trees with sparrows'

■ FIGURE 3.7 *An after-church Sunday stroll in the Square, shown here in the 1880s, was begun with the opening of the Church of the Holy Trinity in 1859.* (The Historical Society of Pennsylvania [HSP], *Stroll on the Square.*)

nests in the daytime, mark them, and at night go and gather them in. The old ladies were aghast at such slaughter, but many will hold that aught tending to decimate the English sparrow was to be encouraged.[35]

The same illusion of autonomy made the Square a preferred venue for courting couples. Because the Square was presumed to be monitored by respectable residents watching from their windows, young single women, now out in society, were apparently permitted to stroll the Square's red gravel walks with their beaux unchaperoned in the afternoons. Here a romance might develop as they paused to admire one of the fountains or to sit on one of the Square's newly installed benches.

The primary check on their behavior came not from adults but from the children playing nearby. A girl named Mae Townsend Pease later recalled that she and her Uncle Charlie "never were fond of each other after I had seen him sitting in Rittenhouse Square one day with a young lady. I stopped my game of tag and led all my playmates in single file past the bench where he was sitting, chanting, 'Uncle Charlie has a best girl.' He told Mother that I was an ill-mannered brat and should be punished."[36]

By 1858 the neighborhood around the Square had grown sufficiently prestigious to attract John Edgar Thomson—president of the Pennsylvania Railroad, then the world's largest corporation—who moved with his wife to a house at the corner of Eighteenth and Spruce streets, in the process becoming the first in a line of Pennsylvania Railroad presidents who lived on or near the Square.[37]

Two other prominent arrivals in the early 1860s suggest that by then the Square's reputation had spread beyond Philadelphia. Robert Sturgis was a Bostonian who amassed a fortune in the China trade. By the time he and his wife, Susan, settled on Walnut Street in 1862, Sturgis had retired at the age of thirty-four.[38] Their house on Walnut Street stood two doors west of James Harper's mansion, but they bought it not from Harper—who had sold his lots ten years earlier—but from a developer who had put up three homes along Walnut.[39] In this spacious house over the next thirty-eight years, Susan Sturgis—ten years younger than her husband—raised four daughters, who became known in Philadelphia society as "the beautiful Sturgis sisters," and three sons.[40]

The Sturgis family was just the sort James Harper had envisioned on Walnut Street when he first bought up the block a generation earlier. By contrast, another resident, Sarah Josepha Hale, filled a category that James Harper could never have imagined: She was a career woman—a widow with a family to support (Figure 3.8). Like the Sturgises, Mrs. Hale came from Boston, where she had edited the *Ladies Magazine* and achieved some fame as the author of the children's poem "Mary Had a Little Lamb" as well as the first person to propose Thanksgiving Day as a national holiday. When the *Ladies Magazine* merged with *Godey's Lady's Book* in 1837, she moved with it to Philadelphia, and over the next forty years she built *Godey's* into America's leading women's literary and fashion periodical, with 150,000 subscribers nationwide. Mrs. Hale settled in a house at 1826 Rittenhouse Square, where her daughter conducted a school for young ladies.

Mrs. Hale was a civic-minded woman who used her pen to advocate her causes, and the care of public squares was one of them. The object of public squares, she wrote in 1853,

is to get as unextended a line of uninterrupted promenade as is possible within the given limits. . . . If the inclosure

■ FIGURE 3.8 *Sarah Josepha Hale, a resident of 1826 Rittenhouse Square, was a founder of Vassar College and a champion of women's education. She was also the editor of* Godey's Lady's Book, *the most widely read women's magazine in America.*
(Print and Picture Collection, Free Library of Philadelphia.)

is small, the rapid succession of angles and turns becomes extremely disagreeable, and continually breaks in upon the *pas des promeneurs*, the conversations of a party, or individual contemplation.[41]

Mrs. Hale objected, for example, to an 1841 ordinance that prohibited walking on the grass or climbing on trees, which she felt caused undue hardship to poor children "who are obliged to remain during this oppressive [summer] season in the city."[42] Many summer illnesses, she contended, "are owing to the want of places where these young beings can have free exercise and fresh air."[43] The "freedom of the public squares," she argued, meant not "the freedom merely, of the hot, dry, gravel walks—but the unrestricted enjoyment of the green grass, the luxury of walking and playing under the shade of the noble trees."[44] Her crusading voice helped articulate a vision of public squares as public resources for children's health.

ONE FACTOR THAT distinguished Rittenhouse Square's new arrivals from other Philadelphians was their method of traveling from one place to another. By the 1850s, Philadelphia's streets were clogged with four hundred horse-drawn hacks and cabs (carriages for hire), and more than three hundred horse-drawn omnibuses plied their trade, not to mention dozens of horse-drawn sleighs in the winter. As the city's population shifted west, these public conveyances increasingly extended across Broad Street to the western outskirts of the city, including Rittenhouse Square. These vehicles shared the road with wagons delivering bread and peddling produce and oysters.

In a growing city, the speed, comfort, and convenience of a private carriage increasingly appealed to those who could afford it. By the late 1850s, horses probably occupied more space around the Square than people did. James Harper had five stables and a two-story carriage house behind his Walnut Street home. William Divine was known to favor fast horses and horse racing after he became a gentleman with a home on Rittenhouse Square. Joseph Harrison built an entire block of stables along Chancellor Street behind his Harrison Row, a group of brownstone houses on Locust Street that shared a common garden as well (an idea he had picked up while traveling in major European cities). The Sturgis family kept stables on Delancey Street. Others, less pecunious, rented stables in the neighborhood.

What J. P. Morgan later said about yachts—"If you must ask how much it costs, you can't afford to own one"—applied to private carriages as well. George Fahnestock of Seventeenth Street discovered as much in 1862 after his invalid wife was traumatized in a hired carriage whose inebriated driver almost turned the carriage over. Mrs. Fahnestock escaped injury, but her bonnet box was thrown off, "trodden underfoot," as Fahnestock put it, completely demolished, and left in the street.[45]

Rather than risk such an experience again, Fahnestock decided to buy his own carriage and horses. He found that the affluence of the times had created a seller's market in Philadelphia, and at Watson's Carriage Depository on Thirteenth Street new carriages were back-ordered for a year. Even in New York, Fahnestock's choices were limited, but for $1,400 he finally purchased a vehicle that Fahnestock found handsome, "although too showy for our taste."

Of course the carriage was useless without horses. "It seems impossible to find anything now," Fahnestock complained. "They buy up all the horses, carriages, drivers, stables and everything else." He eventually had to go to Baltimore to buy two horses.

The next challenge was finding a parking place (some things never change). The most convenient stable had a waiting list, and Fahnestock was forced to stable farther away. Ultimately he decided to build his own stable, a project that consumed a year and cost far more than he had budgeted.

Even then Fahnestock's carriage project was not finished. He still needed fur driving gloves and an India rubber overcoat for the coachman, a robe of wolverine skins for the passengers, and a harness set and covers for the horses.

At last it seemed Mrs. Fahnestock could go out in style, comfort, and safety. Yet within two months, one of Fahnestock's horses was frightened by a passing coal cart, causing the cart to run its shaft through Fahnestock's new carriage. Now he confronted repair bills and the necessity to go horse shopping once again.

That Rittenhouse Square abounded in private carriages is testimony to the neighborhood's growing affluence. Fairman Rogers drove his own four-in-hand coach and tandem team—an impressive driving skill—and wrote the definitive manual on coaches and coaching, filled with such advice to his gentlemanly audience as "If a man has not hands enough to spare one to take off his hat to bow to a lady, he should continue to practice driving until he can find one" (Figure 3.9).[46]

To be sure, less elegant private conveyances could be found, but these still required horses and stables. For the vast majority of Philadelphians as the city expanded, public transportation was critical to getting around. Despite widespread fears of danger, congestion, and noise, a new horse-drawn streetcar railway system was launched in the early 1860s, making Rittenhouse Square much more accessible to the business district around Third Street, about a mile to the east. By 1861 a horse-drawn trolley route operated on Walnut Street from the Delaware River to the Schuylkill. Within a year of its opening, the project was declared a success; more shoppers than ever flooded the streets, and real estate values rose.

The horsecars were indisputably noisy. In addition to the hooves of two big horses on the cobblestones, the horses wore bells on their necks that "could be heard a block away," according to Mae Pease, who lived on Chestnut Street.[47] Eventually the horsecar companies agreed to a Sunday compromise: They would not operate until one in the afternoon, remove bells, walk horses past churches, and avoid other unnecessary noise.[48] In this manner the worshippers at Holy Trinity and St. James (at Twenty-first and Walnut) and other churches along the Walnut Street line were able to worship undisturbed.[49]

Yet Philadelphia was on its way to a horsedrawn-streetcar system that by 1880 would involve thirteen railways, twelve hundred cars, and seven thousand horses

and mules—and, with them, a civic problem more noxious than noise. Each horse deposited ten pounds of manure daily on Philadelphia's streets. Alighting from a Walnut Street car at Eighteenth Street on his way home from work in the 1860s, Henry Cohen knew to step carefully. Women passengers learned to raise their long skirts. For the first time, street sanitation became a major civic issue.

In the winter, streets around the Square were likely to be even more precarious. The street railway companies salted the tracks to melt the snow and ice, leaving residents to cope with a wretched mix of mud, salt, and snow.

■ FIGURE 3.9 *Mr. and Mrs. Fairman Rogers in their coach in Fairmount Park. The Rogers family built a house at 202 South Nineteenth Street that was later occupied by Alexander Cassatt.*
(*The Fairman Rogers Four-in-Hand*, Thomas Eakins. Courtesy of the Philadelphia Museum of Art: gift of William Alexander Dick, 1930.)

The diarist Sidney Fisher, who generally waxed enthusiastic about the convenience and mobility of the new horse-car system, also prophetically intuited that the price of the prosperity generated by the new transportation would be the destruction of the cozy way of life enjoyed by his class. As railways encouraged Philadelphians to live in distant suburbs, he predicted, "before long, town life, life in close streets and alleys, will be confined to a few occupations, and cities will be mere collections of shops, warehouses, factories and places of business."[50] There seemed no reason to think that Rittenhouse Square could resist such a force.

ALL THE COURTING and cavorting on Rittenhouse Square in the early 1860s was played out against the backdrop of the Civil War. Before the outbreak of the war in 1861, Philadelphians had been divided and apathetic on the subject of slavery. The South was one of the city's best customers, and Philadelphia in turn used Southern products such as lumber, turpentine, and cotton. Hundreds of Southern students attended Philadelphia's medical colleges. Although Quakers had organized America's first antislavery society even before the revolution, by 1861 the city's defenders of racial equality were in a distinct minority. When John Brown's body passed through Philadelphia on December 4, 1859, a mob reacted by holding a proslavery demonstration at the Broad and Prime Street (later Washington Avenue) railroad station.[51]

After the outbreak of the Civil War in 1861, Rittenhouse Square became a military parade ground. Here the troops of the University Light Infantry (later Artillery), organized by the University of Pennsylvania's literary department, held its drills, "the iron gates being closed so we could make our maneuvers without interference," the unit's sergeant, John Cadwalader, later recalled (Figure 3.10).[52]

In 1862, Holy Trinity hired as its pastor the Reverend Phillips Brooks, a young New Englander who had studied at Virginia Theological Seminary, where

he became radicalized by the experience of witnessing slavery firsthand. In Philadelphia, Brooks helped found a "colored" Sunday school at Thirteenth and Race streets. Brooks unequivocally attacked "the hateful curse of slavery" from his pulpit. "Its existence in the South and its approval in the North," he declared, "is the great crushing, cursing sin of our national life and the cause of all our evils."[53]

■ Figure 3.10 *An artist's rendering, circa 1863, of the University of Pennsylvania Light Infantry drilling in the Square. The gates around the Square were closed during these maneuvers.*

When Brooks arrived, Holy Trinity was more or less evenly divided between Union and Southern sympathizers. Judge George Washington Woodward, a founder of Holy Trinity, withdrew from its vestry and offered his pew for sale, complaining in a speech, "We must reassert the right of slaveholders." Another congregant named Vaux sold his pew because, he said, he was not black enough to worship at Holy Trinity.[54]

Brooks did in fact lose several parishioners with his abolitionist sermons. But he gained more followers than he lost in the process. "Both afternoon and evening were overcrowded," he boasted in a letter to his parents in 1862. "Our Wednesday evening lectures are always more than full. . . . We are doing well, and have every reason to hope for the future."[55] (It was not only his preaching that filled the pews; Brooks also attracted the mothers of marriageable-age daughters, who envisioned the handsome young pastor as a suitable son-in-law.)

As Brooks continued to preach against slavery, his reputation for courage and eloquence grew. At a time when preachers and other orators constituted a prime source of public entertainment, Holy Trinity was always crowded when Brooks preached; often chairs were set up in the aisles to accommodate overflow crowds. But he was much more than a preacher: Following a trip to the Holy Land after the Civil War, Brooks wrote the poem "O Little Town of Bethlehem," which Holy Trinity's organist, Lewis Redner, set to music and which became a classic Christmas carol. His example provides the first hint of Rittenhouse Square's emergence as an urban oasis not only in terms of physical surroundings but also as an incubator of ideas and artistic expression.

IN THE SUMMER of 1863, the Confederate army under Robert E. Lee assembled a force of seventy-five thousand men to invade the North. Lee planned to strike into central Pennsylvania, capture the state capital at Harrisburg, cut off

Philadelphia's rail connections to western Pennsylvania's coal fields, and, in the process, exacerbate the pessimism and defeatism already plaguing the demoralized North. In June, Lee's troops were spotted within 150 miles of Philadelphia. Fear and despair pervaded the city.

"To ARMS! The Rebels Are Upon Us!" the *Pennsylvania Inquirer* shouted in a headline.[56]

"Lee's army is at Carlisle," Brooks wrote in his diary on June 28, "only one hundred miles from Philadelphia, and yet the city is perfectly quiet, and a terrible apathy is keeping everyone idle, just waiting to be taken."[57] The next day Mayor Alexander Henry, in an open message to Philadelphians, warned, "The foot of the Rebel is already at the gates of your capital, and unless you arouse to instant action it may in a few days hence cross your own thresholds."[58]

Brooks and a hundred other ministers were among those who had dug trenches and put up earthworks for the city's defense. Henry Cohen, too old for regular duty, joined the Blue Reserves Home Guard. George Fahnestock, who a few years earlier had recorded the complications of buying a carriage, now documented in his diary the prospect of his entire community's destruction:

> *Saturday, June 27th*
> Where this will end I cannot conjecture. The archives and records of the State are loaded in [rail] cars and upon the siding in West Philadelphia.

> *Monday, June 29*
> Mother is greatly excited and has all her servants busy packing clothing and all her valuables which will fill a cart or two.

> *Tuesday, June 30*
> It seems to be the prevailing impression that the rebels will make no attempt towards this city, yet many families have left and still more have sent away their valuables.

Wednesday, July 1

We have not yet decided upon leaving home, where to go, or whether to close the house, or leave a servant or two in charge. These war times are most trying to one's nerves. We scarcely know what cause to pursue.

Even while some families fled the city at the end of June, women and children were arriving in Philadelphia from Harrisburg and points west, "fleeing the desperate battle in progress."[59] On July 1, George Fahnestock wrote in his diary, "In the silence of the night, with nearly all the family abed, I hear the recruiting drums, and the bells of locomotives or their hoarse whistle as trains arrive or depart."

His concentration was interrupted by a knock at the door and the arrival of three children sent by their family "out of harm's way to my care." The children had arrived on the last train out of Chambersburg, only 25 miles west of Gettysburg, where a fierce battle was expected. There, just 140 miles west of Philadelphia, Lee's army of 75,000 was about to confront a Union force of nearly 100,000 commanded by the Philadelphian General George Gordon Meade.

Two sons of the Rittenhouse Square textile manufacturer William Divine were with Meade's army. But probably no one in Philadelphia was more anxious than General Meade's wife, Margaret, who lived at 2037 Pine Street. She awaited news of both her husband and their son, who accompanied his father as his aide. General Meade had reluctantly taken charge of Union forces just four days before the battle, which would, Meade wrote to his wife, "decide the fate of our country and our cause."[60]

4

The Family Years

[1863–1884]

THE FOURTH OF JULY fell on a Saturday in 1863, but anxiety over the battle caused the mayor to cancel all celebrations in Philadelphia. That night found Reverend Phillips Brooks and his Rittenhouse Square neighbor, Henry Cohen, huddled with fellow members of the Union League, an organization that had been founded a year earlier to support the Union cause. George Fahnestock, who had spent much of the day among the crowd waiting for "extras" outside a newspaper office on Third Street, observed that night in his diary:

> A great battle was fought yesterday, in which we gained advantages, and captured 3000 prisoners. The slaughter was fearful on both sides. Our loss was heavy in officers. This day I doubt not will witness an awful conflict—perhaps one of the bloodiest of the war. God grant us a victory, and humble trust in Himself. . . . Reports are abundant, but we have nothing reliable.

By the time of the battle of Gettysburg, South Rittenhouse Square Street had evolved into a fully developed row of tall row houses. The rambunctious white buck was still tethered in the Square, but the Square's lawn had been all but trampled by the drilling of the University of Pennsylvania's Light Infantry. Sunday mornings on Rittenhouse Square and the surrounding streets remained a quiet contrast to the weekday commotion. The usual clatter of horsecars was stilled because service was prohibited until after Sunday worship. This Sunday silence was especially pronounced in the summer, when most residents around the Square shuttered their homes and moved to the country or sailed abroad to escape the heat. This summer, fearing Lee's invasion, even more families than usual had left the city.

Of the people who remained in town that Sunday morning, July 5, the Irish Catholics from the surrounding community gathered at St. Patrick's Church, and the Methodists at Western Methodist (the "Brickmakers' Church"). Most residents of the fine homes on the Square and down Walnut Street who remained in the city would have worshipped at one of the neighborhood's three Episcopal churches: St. Mark's on Locust Street, St. James on Twenty-second above Walnut, or—most likely—Holy Trinity on the Square, where the Reverend Phillips Brooks preached his abolitionist conscience.

A service was in progress at Church of the Holy Trinity that Sunday when the first telegraph reports of a great Union victory began to trickle in to Philadelphia, where they quickly spread by word of mouth. When Henry Cohen got the good news, he was eager to share it with his friend Brooks. Cohen was then fifty-three years old, endowed with billowing white muttonchops and a carefully groomed mustache. He was president of Philadelphia's oldest synagogue, Congregation Mikveh Israel on Seventh Street north of Arch.[1] As a Jew who worshipped on Friday, he was free on Sunday to monitor the latest news while his friend conducted the service at Holy Trinity.

"My father," his son Charles later recalled, "imbued with patriotic fervor and knowing of Mr. Brooks' anxiety, crossed over to the church, entering it at the close of the service, and had the privilege of giving to the rector the welcome news, which Brooks quickly announced to the congregation."[2]

When Henry Cohen returned home from his errand to Holy Trinity that Sunday, he would have seen the darkened windows of his South Rittenhouse Square neighbor Francis M. Drexel, killed just a month before in a freak accident as he alighted from a railroad train.[3] Brooks left Philadelphia the next day to minister to both Union and Confederate troops at Gettysburg. As both men had anticipated, the battle was indeed the turning point in the Civil War. Yet it was also a turning point in the history of Philadelphia and the people who lived around Rittenhouse Square.

WHEN THE WAR ended in 1865 and General Meade returned to Philadelphia, he was given a hero's welcome, returning to a house at Nineteenth Street and Delancey Place that grateful local citizens had presented to his wife, Margaret, during the war.

Meade was not a wealthy man, but his "distinguished patrician bearing" and his pedigree from the notable Meade and Sargent families ensured him a place in the city's civic and social affairs. (Meade cut an imposing figure when he rode his white horse in full uniform through the neighborhood.)[4] Since he was an engineer by training, Meade was appointed to the Fairmount Park Commission in 1867, and he subsequently designed the park's drives, walks, and bridle paths.[5]

But Meade's stature was an exception: In prosperous postwar Philadelphia as elsewhere in the victorious North, the yardstick for status was neither family lineage nor accomplishment but money. Philadelphia changed in character from a port city to a center of manufacturing, commerce, banking, and transportation.[6] The captains of industry brought their new fortunes and young families to homes on Rittenhouse Square and along Walnut and Locust streets.

Now the Cohen family (among others) had many new neighbors with homes and lifestyles much more extravagant than theirs. Henry Cohen's son Charles later recalled that he or any of his classmates "could stand with a snowball on the corner of Rittenhouse Square, any winter morning and take his pick of the top hats of twenty millionaires."[7]

Had any of those boys thrown that snowball in 1867, he might have hit the top hat of Colonel Thomas A. Scott, the Cohens' next-door neighbor to the west. Scott was a self-made man who by 1860 had worked his way up from railroad station agent to first vice president of the Pennsylvania Railroad. During the Civil War, Scott had served as assistant secretary of war in charge of troop movement. When he returned to Philadelphia and the Pennsylvania Railroad, Scott assembled two lots for a winter residence on the Square, just two blocks from the home of J. Edgar Thomson, the railroad's president from 1852 to 1872. At the southeast corner of Nineteenth Street and South Rittenhouse Square, Scott put up a fifty-two-room mansion, with elaborately carved mantels and colorful designs on the walls and ceilings (Figure 4.1).[8] Here Colonel Scott lived with his wife, three children, and twelve servants.[9] By 1874 he was the railroad's president; by the time of his death in 1881 the Pennsylvania Railroad was the world's largest corporation twice over.

Philadelphia's postwar industrial growth—much of it generated by the Pennsylvania Railroad's expansion—"unsettled the whole social system of the city," wrote Alexander McClure, editor of *Old Time Notes* and a frequent commentator on social mores.[10] This shift troubled members of the city's prewar upper class, who had mostly defined themselves by their descent from old families or civic achievements. Often the words "ostentatious" or "new rich" were whispered disparagingly in polite company.

After attending a party in what he allowed were "handsome rooms," the diarist Sidney Fisher noted in his diary on February 1, 1866, "The tone of the party, its general effect, was deficient in refinement, in dignity, in short it was

rather vulgar. And why not? *Business people* are now in society, here as in New York."

Until the Civil War, "our society had been a close corporation, largely professional," lamented Mrs. Frederick Rhinelander Jones, who bore several old distinguished Philadelphia names (she was born Mary Cadwalader Rawle). "Some people had more money than others, as they have always had since the civilised world began, but riches in themselves were no criterion. . . . We all knew each other, and had many small parties."[11]

■ FIGURE 4.1 *Thomas Alexander Scott house. This house, on the southwest corner of South Nineteenth Street, had fifty-two rooms and a ballroom.* (Print and Picture Collection, Free Library of Philadelphia.)

The jeweler J. E. Caldwell, who catered to Philadelphia society, told his friends that after the Civil War there was such extraordinary demand for jewels that it was hard for him to keep up with orders. To his great surprise, he found he no longer knew most of his customers,[12] since many of them were buying their first diamonds.

These people spent their money extravagantly. George Fahnestock, who had struggled to afford his carriage and horses, noted in his diary on December 20, 1864, that "the high prices of goods, and the abundance of money begets an extravagance never before known in this country. . . . [T]he windows are filled with the most expensive goods. The ladies dress in the richest fabrics, and seem to take as many yards for a dress as would carpet a large parlor."[13]

In the post–Civil War years, entertaining became costly, lavish, and "gaudy in awkward decoration."[14] The new moneyed crowd, according to Fisher, "plunged into the most extravagant display in efforts not merely to imitate, but to surpass the hospitality and social distinction of the cultured families of the city." To old Philadelphians, Rittenhouse Square became synonymous with the newly rich industrialists who possessed more money than they knew how to spend tastefully.

"I drove up to the house in 18th St. on the east side of Rittenhouse Square at 2 o'clock . . . ," Fisher confided to his diary after one party in 1868:

> It was all very pleasant, the house is large & handsome, the lunch was excellent, there was no crowd yet the rooms were well filled, & there were some very pretty & two or three beautiful girls. I saw but few familiar faces and thought the tone & manner of the company, as a whole, decidedly inferior to what our society displayed when I was young.[15]

After a reception for the Grand Duke Alexis of Russia at the Academy of Music in 1871, chaired by General Meade, the social critic Alexander McClure reported that "never before or since has there been such a gorgeous display of costly apparel and jewels . . . over-dressed and jewel-spangled women."[16]

The new social order in Philadelphia was perhaps epitomized by two organizations, one for men and one for women. The Rittenhouse Club opened in James Harper's former mansion in 1875 for the purpose of promoting literary, artistic, and antiquarian tastes. Imitating the style of a private English club, the Rittenhouse Club offered the city's leading men a civilized refuge from the harsh commercial world outside. Here business talk was forbidden and intellectual conversation encouraged. The club was known for its Chesapeake Bay terrapin soup, made from terrapins kept in pools in the club's basement to ensure their freshness.

The 1876 U.S. Centennial Exposition was Philadelphia's opportunity to show off its new persona as "workshop of the world," and the composition of the Women's Centennial Executive Committee was telling. Its president was Elizabeth Duane Gillespie, a great-granddaughter of Benjamin Franklin who lived just west of Rittenhouse Square.[17] The driving forces on the committee were Mrs. Edgar Thomson, who lived a block south of the Square, and Mrs. Henry Cohen, who lived on the Square. Of the committee's thirteen members, eight lived in the vicinity of Rittenhouse Square; only two lived east of Broad Street.[18]

The committee was formed three years before the 1876 event, and all socially ambitious women coveted a place on its roster. To raise funds for the Centennial, in March 1873 this committee's members applied their social skills to a fund-raising event held at a private home on the west side of the Square—the first of many such events held in or near the Square. A tent was raised over the large garden to accommodate dinner and dancing. Inside was an art exhibit of items loaned from residents around the Square.

The Centennial Exposition itself was America's first mass tourist event. Despite a heat wave that pushed temperatures in Fairmount Park as high as 100 degrees, its opening day crowd of 186,000 was the largest ever assembled in North America.[19] On the hot nights that followed through much of July, many distinguished foreign visitors sought refuge in the cooler confines of Rittenhouse Square. Here they were entertained by Mrs. Joseph Thomas and her daughters, known for their southern charm as well as their fluency in several languages. As the Thomas women placed chairs on the sidewalk in front of their home on the Square's south side, neighbors attracted by this convivial scene brought their own chairs to join the party, and "many memories were carried away of cordial hospitality," as Charles Cohen recalled.[20]

The Centennial Exposition successfully showcased Philadelphia as a sophisticated, cosmopolitan center. The city was riding a wave of pride, growth, and optimism. And where better to live than on Rittenhouse Square?

IN THE YEARS following the Civil War and continuing into the twentieth century, the area's many schools drew children to the Square. On any weekday morning, the area bustled with children on their way to school and many of their fathers on their way to work. One observer described the foot traffic through the Square as a "ballet."[21]

Several generations of neighborhood boys wended their way across the Square to the DeLancey School at Seventeenth and Delancey or to Episcopal Academy at Locust and Juniper.[22] As they crossed the Square in varying patterns, they were likely to encounter the girls passing in groups toward the Miss Irwins' School to the south of the Square.[23] (Its cofounders, the sisters Agnes and Sophie Irwin, were daughters of the U.S. minister to Denmark and great-granddaughters of Benjamin Franklin. Agnes, for whom the school was subsequently renamed, left in 1894 to become dean of Radcliffe College in Boston.)[24] Romantic tales of "secret trysts" between the older Episcopal boys and Miss Irwin's girls in the Square on their way to school captured the imaginations of younger girls.[25]

Some of the girls were headed for the school run by Sarah Josepha Hale's daughter in the early 1860s on the south side of Rittenhouse Square, one door east of the Cohens.[26] In the 1880s some of the figures would have found their way to Mrs. Farnum's "exclusive" school for little children a few doors east of Sarah Hale's school. Both schools enjoyed the advantage of facing the Square. Mrs. Hale advertised her daughter's school in *Godey's Lady's Book*, noting the location as a special asset for students: "Her house is beautifully situated opposite a large park, which makes the air more salubrious than in the closer parts of the city."[27]

The neighborhood abounded in these "parlor" schools for girls, often run by single ladies. Katherine Cohen, Henry's daughter, attended Miss Dickson's school. Mrs. Rush and her daughter Julia ran a day school on Pine Street.[28] A Miss Hill had a school for young ladies, and a Miss Davis operated a school on Eighteenth Street near Pine.

A world apart from these day schools was the Academy of Notre Dame de Namur on the west side of the Square, a convent boarding and day school, opened in 1866 by a cloistered order of Belgian nuns that traced its origins to the French Revolution (Figure 4.2). Like the Square's other new arrivals, the Sisters of Notre Dame de Namur had moved their convent from Juniper and Filbert streets in search of light and fresh air. As the story goes, when their initial inquiries about purchasing land on the Square met with whiffs of the old anti-Catholic hostility, a neighbor family (possibly that of the newly arrived Joshua Lippincott, descendant of an old Philadelphia Quaker family) assisted the nuns. Two sisters were permitted to doff their habits and, with the aid of borrowed clothes and bonnets, presented themselves as ordinary matrons who purchased the property under the family name of the order's founder, Julia Billiart.[29]

Notre Dame's students (including the future actress Ethel Barrymore) were mostly secluded behind the convent's massive double doors and dressed in identical gingham uniforms and brown shoes.

Another excellent girls' school was operated by a daughter of one of Philadelphia's most prominent Jewish families. Miriam Gratz Mordecai, who lived on the south side of the Square, was the daughter of Major Alfred Mordecai (an 1823

graduate of West Point), niece of the philanthropist Rebecca Gratz (immortalized as the model for a character in Walter Scott's *Ivanhoe*), and herself a board member of the Hebrew Sunday School Society. The school run by Miriam and her sister functioned first at Nineteenth and Spruce streets and later on Delancey Place.[30]

AFTER THE EARLY MORNING commuters were settled in their schoolrooms or businesses, activity on the Square paused each day before the entrance of the preschool set. At about 10:00 A.M., nursemaids pushing baby carriages made their appearances (Figure 4.3). The scene described by Constance O'Hara a generation later was actually a throwback to the 1880s.

■ FIGURE 4.3 *Nannies, the real autocrats of the Square, circa 1880.* (Print and Picture Collection, Free Library of Philadelphia.)

A few French governesses kept to themselves, excluding the lone *Fraulein*. The Irish maids constituted the real autocracy of the Square, keeping the colored girls firmly in their place. The Irish nursemaids were fearful snobs—a Celtic characteristic—and their aristocratic young charges, who were often horrid little brats, were bragged about shamelessly to the other maids, as well as the heathen doings of their parents.[31]

Then the relative quiet would be broken by the arrival of the boys from Rittenhouse Academy at Eighteenth and Chestnut, escorted by their principal, Dr. Barrows, who brought the whole school to the Square for recess every morning.[32]

From the time school let out until the custodian locked the iron gates at sundown, the Square belonged to the youngsters.[33] Many years later, when he was

THE FAMILY YEARS
[1863–1884]

eighty, the Philadelphia lawyer and U.S. Senator George Pepper recalled his own rites of passage there in the 1870s:

> I associate with the place the first thrill of loyalty that I ever experienced. Some twenty or thirty boys were wont to gather in the square astride velocipedes and primitive bicycles. We organized a troop and one of our number was chosen captain. One day somebody started a mutiny and tried to persuade some of us to secede from the organization. Our captain faced the hesitating crowd, reminded us that we had chosen him leader and called on us to follow where he led. He then wheeled about and started across the square. I shall never forget the flame of enthusiasm which instantly swept through me as we all wheeled into line behind him. I think it must have been of the same sort that Napoleon enkindled in Marshal Ney.[34]

A custodian named Dandy Stokes was known to lock the gates on people crossing the Square at dusk and enforce strict standards even in broad daylight, much to the annoyance of some boys (Figure 4.4). "During hours of access," Pepper recalled, "the place [Rittenhouse Square] was made pretty nearly intolerable for children by a custodian who kept us off the grass, sprinkled ashes on our ice slides and in general interfered with the normal use of the place as a playground for the children of the neighborhood."[35]

Girls played on the Square too. Mae Pease remembered feeling sorry for her cousin Mathilde because "she was surrounded by maids and governesses and was never allowed to play tag in Rittenhouse Square, where Uncle Dick wanted me to take her. Aunt Minnie considered me a bad influence and never let her play with me and my friends in the Square."[36]

Within their families' townhouses and mansions, the children of Rittenhouse Square enjoyed the benefits of large rooms, high ceilings, private gardens, and

staffs of servants. The Cohen family had two Irish servant girls, the Scott family had twelve resident servants, and the Sturgis family had four single women (from Maryland, France, Denmark, and Ireland) living with them. On Walnut Street, the Alexander Brown family (of the Brown Brothers investment house) lived in John Hare Powel's house with eight live-in servants (four men and four women) to serve just three family members.[37]

Mae Pease, whose grandparents lived in a large (and typical) brownstone house on Walnut Street, remembered:

> There was a big garden in the back with a fountain. The household consisted of my grandparents, two uncles, Uncle Dick and Uncle Charlie, and my Aunt Pauline. The family had a chambermaid, a cook and a colored butler, Odin, who had been born a slave and was an important member of the household. A laundress also came for one dollar a day on Mondays and Tuesdays.[38]

The cost of servants, one Walnut Street resident recalled, was negligible:

A good cook could be had for one dollar and fifty cents per week, and a professed cook, able to make jellies and trifle, received one dollar and seventy-five cents a week. A waitress and a chambermaid cost each one dollar and twenty-five cents a week, and a manservant not more than from twelve to fifteen dollars a month. Our washing was done in the country and our ironing at home.[39]

"To those whose good fortune it was to have lived around Rittenhouse Square and looked from their windows upon it," a resident named George Brinton recalled years later, "the memory of those primeval forest trees, refreshing to the eye in the summer with their splendid foliage and in the winter covered with snow or sparkling ice, will always be a happy thing to dwell upon."[40]

In this manner, the six acres of Rittenhouse Square became inextricably bound to the lives of those wealthy and influential Philadelphians who grew up there—people who were likely, as adults, to use their wealth and influence to defend the Square against any perceived threat.

BUT WHAT OF the "other half"—the working-class English, Irish, and blacks who had settled the neighborhood before the rich arrived, many of whom now worked as servants in the homes on the Square?

Beyond the immediate periphery of the Square and the major streets leading to it, the neighborhood still teemed with children who played in the narrow streets among the carts, carriages, and horsecars. This community lay to the south and west of the Square, between Lombard and Bainbridge, Eighteenth and the Schuylkill River. As in earlier generations, the men worked at the docks on the Schuylkill River or at brickyards, lumberyards, and marble yards or were small craftsmen with shops. The women took in laundry or worked as domestic servants in the new homes on the Square.

The north-south streets of Twentieth and Twenty-first effectively functioned as twin corridors separating the working-class families to the west and south from the upper-class families on Rittenhouse Square. Within this corridor itself dwelled a cluster of middle-class residents who operated their own small businesses. At Twentieth and Lombard streets, Maria Moran had a laundry; May O'Brien, near Twentieth and Locust, was a dressmaker; and Ed McKeown, on South Twenty-first Street, was a printer.[41]

Some children of these middle- and working-class families attended St. Patrick's parochial school on Twentieth Street, which had an enrollment of nine hundred students by 1880. Some attended Southwest Public School at Lombard and Twenty-first streets. Many of these people—adults and children alike—crisscrossed the Square on their way to work.

Two blocks south of Rittenhouse Square was "the vast, vague 'colored' section," as the lawyer (and later U.S. attorney general) Francis Biddle described it.[42] The strip west of Seventeenth Street from Spruce Street south to Lombard was one of the best and oldest residential sections in the city for African Americans. Perhaps three thousand relatively prosperous black people, many descended from freedmen of the previous century, were crammed into small streets like Addison, Rodman, and Waverly, as well as the broader Lombard.[43] Although most of these African American residents worked as laborers and domestic servants, many were entrepreneurs; several were well-respected caterers.[44] They were self-employed if only because of white employers' prejudices.

"One has but to notice the coachmen on the driveways or the butlers on Rittenhouse Square, or the nursemaids, to see how white servants have displaced Negroes," the black sociologist W.E.B. DuBois complained. "A white butler on Rittenhouse Square sums up the situation. You see they go to Europe and bring home Englishmen, and that knocks out the Negro."[45]

THE CHILDREN OF nearby working-class families enjoyed grudging access to the Square year-round, but they had it largely to themselves in the summers, when the Square's immediate residents left town to escape the city heat. For those "without a nurse or governess in sight," the lawyer (and U.S. attorney general) Francis Biddle later perceptively observed, the Square "in the drooping heat of a dusty August day was dirty and human."[46] A passerby might have seen a "little black girl, her pigtails tied with a single cherry-colored ribbon, . . . emerging north along 20th Street, accompanied by an immense lean cat . . . walking past the great shuttered houses of the white folk" to play on the Square on a summer's day.[47]

After the intense heat of the long summer days subsided in September, coaches and wagons arrived and shutters reopened, signaling the arrival of fall and, with it, the return of the Square's winter residents.

Once again on bright fall Sundays, as bells broke the morning silence on the Square, the congregations of St. Mark's, Holy Trinity, St. James's, and the Presbyterian Church at Twenty-first and Walnut streets all merged into an informal promenade along the south side of Walnut. "They made upon the onlooker an impression of urbanity, of social experience and of entire self-satisfaction," Pepper recalled. "If during church-time they had confessed themselves miserable sinners, by the time they appeared on parade their restoration to divine favor was seemingly complete."[48]

It was entertainment for spectators as well as for the participants, especially at Easter. In Rittenhouse Square, according to one observer, "not one of the benches were vacant. Spectators were there early that they might miss no part of the parade. The windows of the Rittenhouse Club were crowded with members who had come early to obtain a choice vantage seat."[49] Recalled another, "The men dressed in cutaway coats, striped trousers, grey spats and gloves, top hats and carrying canes, the women in their Easter finery and heavily bunched."[50] When the walk around the Square was finished, "then everyone went visiting . . . whole families, stopping in from house to house to pay their respects" (Figure 4.5).[51]

The "business people" scorned by Sydney Fisher had arrived. The parvenus of 1866 had become the social arbiters of the 1880s.[52]

■ FIGURE 4.5 *Christmas morning on Rittenhouse Square, circa 1886, shortly after the fence was removed. The contrast between the imperious strollers and the two wistful, tattered children (on the right) provided a Victorian metaphor for the Square.*
(Print and Picture Collection, Free Library of Philadelphia.)

WHEN THE CIVIL WAR ended, Rittenhouse Square was not yet the city's preeminent upper-class enclave. Logan Square, north of Market Street, attracted its share of industrial millionaires and gentlefolk to the stately brownstones surrounding that square. But beginning in 1881 the Pennsylvania Railroad constructed sixteen elevated tracks along Market Street from the Schuylkill River to the huge new Broad Street Station across from City Hall. The tracks ran on a viaduct atop a high wall that effectively isolated the north side of Market Street from the south. This infamous "Chinese wall" was an aesthetic horror: high, grimy, coated with soot, and punctuated by dark culverts that seemed to drip noxious fluids. With the arrival of the Chinese wall, Logan Square found itself effectively isolated from the residential neighborhoods south of Market Street. Rittenhouse Square became, beyond question, the "right" side of the tracks (Figure 4.6).

■ FIGURE 4.6 *The Pennsylvania Railroad's ten-block "Chinese wall," built in 1881, isolated Logan Square on the north, thus ensuring the primacy of Rittenhouse Square to the south. The wall, razed in the mid-1950s, is shown here in the 1940s.*
(Print and Picture Collection, Free Library of Philadelphia.)

Alexander Cassatt (Figure 4.7), who lived along the Square at 202 South Nineteenth Street, rose to the presidency of the Pennsylvania Railroad by 1899. Under his leadership, the "Pennsy" would initiate electrification and invade the rival New York Central Railroad's turf by tunneling under the Hudson River into the heart of Manhattan, where the railroad built the legendary Pennsylvania Station. Yet ultimately the railroad would prove the undoing of Rittenhouse Square. After residing around Rittenhouse Square for much of the nineteenth century in reticent, tidy brownstone townhouses, members of Philadelphia's close-knit upper-class community began to purchase summer retreats on old Welsh Quaker farms along the Pennsylvania Railroad's Main Line. As the railroad encouraged its executives to purchase suburban property, this initial trickle soon gave way to

■ Figure 4.7
A portrait of Alexander Cassatt and his son Kelso painted by Alexander's sister, Mary Stevenson Cassatt.

(*Portrait of Alexander J. Cassatt*, Mary Stevenson Cassatt. Courtesy of the Philadelphia Museum of Art: purchased with the W. P. Wilstach Fund and with funds contributed by Mrs. William Coxe Wright, 1959.)

the building of vast year-round estates on a grand scale, an exodus that would continue until the eve of the Great Depression of the 1930s.[53]

Eventually the Main Line would displace Rittenhouse Square as the fashionable place for Philadelphians to live. The Square would survive only by reinventing itself yet again.

The Encroaching City

[1884–1913]

In March 1884, Philadelphia's two legislative bodies, the Select and Common Councils, announced a "plan for the improvement of Rittenhouse Square." In order to better accommodate the city's growing traffic of horsecars, carriages, and ambulances, streets around the Square were to be widened to thirty-six feet, and seventy-four treasured street trees, as well as the iron fence surrounding the Square, were to be removed.

To its proponents, the plan was a logical response to urban congestion: Thanks to its "golden triangle" of coal, iron, and railroads, Philadelphia had become America's industrial hub, and its population had soared from 568,000 in 1860 to 800,000 in 1880.[1] But the proposed plan struck most Rittenhouse Square neighbors as a threat to their way of life.

Already James Harper's home on Walnut Street had been converted to the Rittenhouse Club—the first nonresidential property on the Square since the brickyards had operated there two generations earlier (Figure 5.1). The Pennsylvania

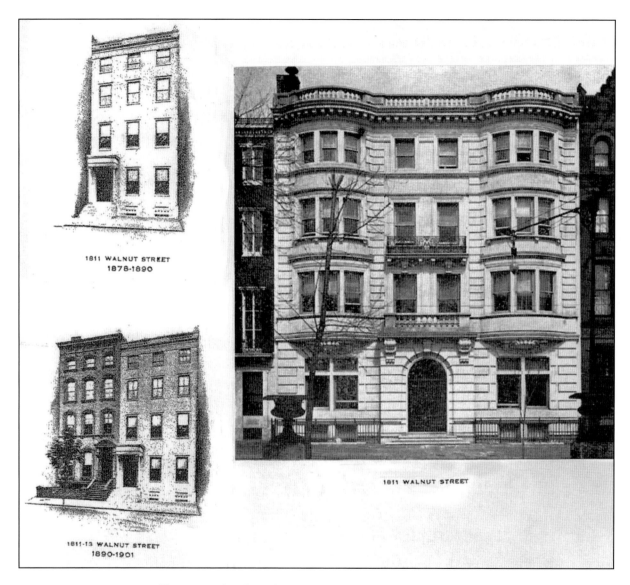

1811 WALNUT STREET
1878-1890

1811-13 WALNUT STREET
1890-1901

1811 WALNUT STREET

■ FIGURE 5.1 *Rittenhouse Club. This picture shows the evolution of the building: James Harper's house and his daughter's house next door were joined in 1902, and a beaux arts facade was created to form the Rittenhouse Club as seen today.*

Railroad's new line to Chestnut Hill was encouraging many residents of the Square to move to that quaint "suburb within the city," where some Square residents already had summer homes. The proposed new traffic patterns seemed likely to hasten this exodus. The result could be the destruction of life on Rittenhouse Square as its residents had known it.

By 1884, the Square's "founding fathers"—Philip Physick, John Hare Powel, James Harper, William Divine, Joseph Harrison, Thomas Scott, and Henry Cohen—were all dead. In some cases their formidable widows—most notably Matilda Cohen, Anna Scott, and Mrs. J. Edgar Thomson—still survived. All the supposed prestige and influence of the Square and its residents seemed to count for little with the city's two Common Councils, whose newer members no longer respected the old names and who had other more pressing priorities in any case.

"If the Commissioner of Public Property would extend his walks as far as West Rittenhouse Square," complained one anonymous Rittenhouse Square woman in a letter to the *Evening Bulletin* that February, "he would see the results of his efforts to clean one portion of the city at the expense of another by his act of removing the snow and dirt from the State House [later Independence Hall] pavements and placing it in huge piles in the Square, to lie for months, until the spring sun shall have power to melt them. . . . The present condition of the Square is a disgrace to the city, an eyesore to the residents in the neighborhood, and will probably be productive of sickness and disease."[2]

In the absence of systematic snow removal, the iron gates to the Square were often locked in winter until accumulations of snow were sufficiently melted. During such weeks, Charles Cohen later recalled, "our chief amusement was to decide the depth of the snow, it being measured by the small round-topped wooden stools."[3]

The city's two Councils had properly focused on the larger and immediate needs of a relentlessly growing city; to their members, the Square was above all an obstruction to the orderly flow of traffic through the heart of a great city, not to mention an onerous expense (the Councils' resolution also called for reducing the

Square's maintenance costs by replacing its gravel walks with asphalt). But to the Square's residents, the greater challenge lay in preserving their genteel, humane enclave for the benefit of future generations.

The question was how, precisely, to respond. At the time, no formal civic advocacy organizations existed. Citizens with civic complaints met informally, wrote petitions and presented them to the City Councils, and then disbanded until the next crisis.

To be sure, Rittenhouse Square residents of both genders had already begun banding together to create a variety of civic and cultural institutions and clubs where ideas, once exchanged, might be translated into political action. The Philadelphia Museum of Art was opened in Memorial Hall in Fairmount Park in 1877 as an outgrowth of the Centennial. The Pennsylvania Academy of the Fine Arts was in its period of highest national prestige. Small private groups for both men and women were being organized around common interests, like the Racquet Club (founded in 1859) and the Penn Club (1875), soon to be followed by the Contemporary Club (1886), the Art Club (1887), the Sketch Club (1889), the Browning Society (1894), and the Geographic Society (1897).

Like Matilda Cohen, Anna Scott was a widow who had lived on the south side of Rittenhouse Square for many years, had raised her children there, and wanted to preserve the Square as she had known it. Both women had been involved in the Women's Committee of the 1876 Centennial, Matilda Cohen as one of its organizers and Anna Scott as a contributor of many items to the fund-raising exhibition.

Mrs. J. Edgar Thomson, who had lived on the northeast corner of Eighteenth and Spruce streets since 1858, had worked with both women as treasurer of the Centennial Loan Exhibition. As spouses of Pennsylvania Railroad executives, Mrs. Thomson and Mrs. Scott had known each other for many years.[4]

Together in March 1884 these three women organized a meeting about the Council proposals that became a model for many similar civic meetings into the twenty-first century. Their chosen venue was the home of the investment banker Alexander Brown, who lived in the house on Walnut Street that John Hare Powel had built in 1840 but had rarely occupied. Each of its two parlors was crowded that night, mostly with elderly people who had moved to Rittenhouse Square at midcentury and had raised their families there.[5]

When the meeting came to order, it quickly became clear that opinions varied. The Councils' proposal included asphalting paths and widening them to extend Locust and Nineteenth streets (which the Square interrupted) as pedestrian thoroughfares, removing the iron railing, and widening the surrounding streets. Some speakers at the meeting favored a granite or asphalt walk diagonally across the square, leaving the other paths gravel. Some wanted a lower railing around the Square; some wanted no fence at all; while still others wanted the existing railing painted and gilded.[6]

But by the end of the meeting the group had reached some consensus. A subsequent petition signed by 1,196 residents (Mrs. Thomson the first) asked the Select and Common Councils to reconsider their recently passed ordinances to alter Rittenhouse Square.[7]

The petitioners acknowledged the Councils' concerns for traffic and costs but stressed the Square's unique function as a "health-preserving resort" within the city. The Square, they argued, offered city residents a respite from summer heat—and gravel was cooler than asphalt. "Thousands of children" who played on the Square, they added, could be injured by falls on hard asphalt paths. Without the iron railing around the Square, they contended, "bulls, cows, and other savage animals would then have access to it."[8] As for the loss of seventy-four street trees that would result from the widening of the streets, their petition said,

> We entreat you to think of the hundreds of children who play daily under the shade of those trees, and those especially who cannot leave the city during the great heat. We implore you to think of the many poor women

from stifling alleys who bring their sickly children there by daybreak, in hopes that they may be revived by the cooler air afforded by those very trees now doomed to destruction. Will you not consent to save from the ruthless axe God's work of fifty years, that His poor may enjoy them still?

For all its eloquence, the petition was only partially successful. The Councils proceeded with their plan to remove the iron railing, and the Square's narrow gravel walkways were replaced with wide asphalt paths. But the 1884 petition probably prevented the widening of the streets around the Square.[9]

After the iron fence was removed, pedestrians did, in fact, occasionally encounter sheep or steers that had strayed as they were being driven to slaughterhouses on the Schuylkill in the night hours when the streets were empty.

But as things turned out, the new asphalt paths offered more benefits than liabilities, at least for children. The very innovations that parents had feared, far from deterring children at play, were exploited by children in ways their parents had not anticipated. Skinned knees notwithstanding, children loved the asphalt because it made roller-skating possible for the first time. And the emergence of adults on the Square as a civic force helped preserve the Square's character intact for another generation and more. The landscaping done at this time, the removal of the much-maligned fountains, and installation of some cast-iron urns on granite pedestals were all the major improvements that would be undertaken until 1913.[10]

THE GRANDCHILDREN OF Francis M. Drexel, the immigrant patriarch of the great banking family, returned to Rittenhouse Square from West Philadelphia with their inherited wealth at the end of the century, following the death in 1893 of the greatest of the banking Drexels, Anthony J. Drexel, Sr.[11] By the 1890s, five Drexel families lived on the Square.[12]

Anthony Drexel's daughter, Sarah "Sally" Drexel Fell Van Rensselaer, was described by her niece Cordelia Drexel Biddle as "a small, gay, witty woman with the brightest blue eyes I've ever seen [Figure 5.2]. We were so happy being with her we romped, galloped, and stuffed ourselves with abandon."[13] In 1898, following the death of her first husband, John Fell, three years earlier, Sarah and her new husband, Alexander Van Rensselaer, razed the William Lejée house (built in 1849), at the northwest corner of Eighteenth and Walnut streets, a property that was once a James Harper investment.[14] In its place they built what one historian described as a "marble monument to the luxurious life of inherited wealth and high fashion." (Among its remaining features are a stained glass dome and ninety-four images of the doges of Venice that looked down from the drawing room ceiling.)[15]

■ FIGURE 5.2 *Sarah Drexel Fell Van Rensselaer and her husband built the grand mansion on the northwest corner of Eighteenth and Walnut streets.* (Temple University Libraries, Urban Archives, Philadelphia, Pennsylvania.)

The mansion's style stood in contrast to the row of brick houses in the center of that Walnut Street block and even to the villa style of the earlier Physick and Powel houses facing each other across Nineteenth Street on Walnut. It was said to be "one of the most patrician examples" of beaux arts classicism,[16] a style from Europe, especially France, that was gaining popularity in the United States and would exert a profound influence on development on Rittenhouse Square and in Philadelphia a generation later.

Popular history of the time suggests that everyone living within this charmed area, if not as closely related to each other as the Drexels, knew each other. In

Cordelia Drexel Biddle's "huge brownstone" near Twenty-first and Walnut, her family had a dining room that could seat forty. Dinner parties there, she recalled, started with a list of relatives: "The table was almost filled with Cassatts, Devereuxs, Cadwaladers, Mills, Van Rensselaers, Munns, Fells, Drexels, and Biddles."[17] In his classic account of Philadelphia neighborhoods, the sociologist Digby Baltzell contended, "At no other time in the city's history, before or since, have so many wealthy and fashionable families lived so near one another."[18]

But for that very reason, Philadelphia society often became synonymous with provincialism and complacency. "I believe in the Pennsylvania Railroad, the Republican Party and all good bonds," was this group's mantra. William Bullitt's novel, *It's Not Done*, transparently based on Philadelphia around this time, created a sensation at its publication in 1926. In the novel, the fictitious Aunt Muriel asks rhetorically,

> Is there any other city of a million in the world in which every one who counts lives in an area three streets by eight surrounding a Sacred Square? I've been away twenty years and I'll wager I can tell you every person you've met at dinner in the interval and that there'll be no one I'll meet while I'm here who'll not call me by my first name.

These Philadelphians, Aunt Muriel continues, "still refuse to admit the existence of New York . . . except as a convenience: a place to keep theatrical troupes and ladies who are no better than they should be."[19]

Cordelia Biddle corroborated this fictional attitude in her memoir:

> Even in my time, Philadelphians considered trips to New York as slumming. Just to show their disdain for the parvenus and upstarts of Manhattan, they carefully refrained from taking their dress suits along on their

semi-annual visits. I think it's accurate to say that Philadelphia in those days was a backwater of safety, a happy withdrawal from the world. There was everywhere a feeling of permanence and stability [Figure 5.3].[20]

These impressions were reinforced by Henry James, that quintessential chronicler of New York's Gilded Age, who often sought refuge in the gentility of Rittenhouse Square as his own Washington Square in New York was yielding to the advance of commercial progress. Standing at one of the "ample, tranquil" bay windows of what had been James Harper's house and was now the Rittenhouse Club, James looked south and saw "the large residential square that lay before me shine in its native light. This light, remarkably tender, I thought, for that of a winter afternoon matched with none other I had ever seen."[21]

Then James allowed his eye to rest contentedly upon

the little marble steps and lintels and cornices and copings, all the clear, so placed accents of the good prose text of the mildly purple house across the Square, which seemed to wear them, as all the others did, up and down the streets, in the manner of nice white stockings, neckties, collars, cuffs

■ FIGURE 5.3 *Walnut Street, circa 1900. The entire north side of the Square is shown, featuring the Van Rensselaer House and the Rittenhouse Club.* (Print and Picture Collection, Free Library of Philadelphia.)

. . . and this was somehow an assurance. . . . I had only to turn round again and see where I was, and how it was, in order to feel everything "come out" under the large friendliness, the ordered charm and perfect peace of the Club, housing me with that *whole* protection the bestowal of which on occasion is the finest grace of the hospitality of American clubs. . . .

Philadelphia, in other words, would not only be a family, she would be a "happy" one. . . . It having been clear to me still, in my charming Club and at my illuminating window, that she couldn't *not* be perfect. She would be, of all goodly villages, the very goodliest, probably, in the world [Figure 5.4].[22]

And so the self-satisfied Philadelphians around Rittenhouse Square entertained each other. For the children of the Drexel-Biddle clan, Christmas dinners were "almost too much of a good thing," Cordelia Biddle recalled. "Because of the family rivalry, we went to a big dinner at Aunt Sally Van Rensselaer's at noon, and an even bigger dinner at Aunt Mary's at night." That would be Mary Drexel, wife of Aunt Sally's brother George Childs Drexel, a dowager whom Cordelia described as a "formidable figure" with "striking blonde hair" and "no sense of humor."[23] She replaced the original house at the corner of Eighteenth and Locust streets with a mansion that survives to this day as the home of the Curtis Institute of Music. Not to be outdone by her sister-in-law, Mary Drexel also had a spectacular drawing-room ceiling, with an allegory of Longfellow's poem *Psalm of Life*, painted by the muralist Edwin Howland Blashfield.

As a child, Cordelia routinely walked with her governess to play in Rittenhouse Square. Years later she recalled this as a walk through a "charmed section"—an impression later reinforced by a commentator who wondered whether Rittenhouse Square could be so satisfyingly attractive, if it were not for the approaches to it. South of Walnut, including Pine, Spruce,

■ Figure 5.4 *"The little marble steps and lintels . . . of the . . . house across the Square." This is the view that greeted Henry James when he looked out the window of the Rittenhouse Club, circa 1904.*

Locust, and between Broad and say Twenty-first Streets, comprises one of the most arresting residential sections of the city. Whether the houses are of the best architecture or no, they have a quaint and distinctive air about them. And the streets seem most properly to lead to the lush green Square.[24]

West of the Square, Cordelia Biddle's own immediate family lived more modestly than her Drexel aunts. The regular Biddle household staff included a cook, a kitchen maid, two chambermaids, a mechanic, and two coachmen. In addition, for their frequent large parties they employed special caterers whose staffs included two butlers, two chefs, eight to ten waiters, and a butler named Chalk to supervise it all.

Looking back, Cordelia recalled the interior of this house as "a nightmare of bad taste":

> Father was addicted to statues and they were everywhere in the house, and by present standards, they would be accounted horrible. Along with dainty French gift pieces, he had Chinese gongs and screens and an entire supply of enormous Italian tables, chairs, and chests.[25]

On the west side of the Square, Constance O'Hara remembered the sitting room of her grandfather's house at Twentieth and Locust, overlooking the garden of the Convent of Notre Dame, where she had gone to school:

> [It was] a bedlam of mahogany and tapestry and marble statuary. There are copies of masterpieces framed in alarmingly bright gilt. Sets of books in rich leather fill the bookcase at the back of the room. Deep carpets suck all sound from footsteps; at night gaslights whistle in ornate chandeliers. A coal fire burns red as roses in the grate this February after-

noon. The curtains, in superimposed layers of velvet, silk and Brussels lace, shut out the pale eastern light.[26]

At the east end of this "charmed section," at 1709 Walnut Street, the family of Elizabeth and Willis Martin lived with her parents, Mr. and Mrs. Sargent Price. The Martin family's Quaker heritage—they traced their roots to a Welsh Quaker landholder in 1684[27]—precluded the baroque splendor of the Van Rensselaer dining room, but the formal style of dining in their Walnut Street home paralleled the sumptuous dinners experienced by Cordelia Biddle. Elizabeth Price Martin cut a formidable figure in her floppy hats and elegantly gloved hands, a fitting exterior for a woman who subsequently became a dynamic force in the city. Marion Martin Rivinus recalled her grandmother seated at the head of the table with a butler standing at attention behind her and a footman at his side:

> The kitchen and servants' hall was on the ground floor, opening into the yard, and directly above were the dining room, breakfast room and pantry. The breakfast room was a bright cheery room at the end of the house overlooking the yard and Moravian Street. To secure privacy the end windows were of stained glass with a number of yellow panes. I thought they were the most beautiful windows in the world. A dumb waiter connected the pantry with the servants' hall and one of our indoor sports was to ride up and down on it. The family did a great deal of entertaining and in those days there were many courses, which accounted for the size of the dumb waiter. Outside the pantry window was a large covered box, in which fresh fruit, milk and other perishables were kept to augment the pantry icebox.[28]

A carriage ride in Fairmount Park for "a sampling of spring water" or a healthful dose of fresh air was a popular alternative to tea taking. At 4:00 every afternoon all manner of equipages could be seen "in front of countless houses, their occupants mounting by way of the marble block arranged for that purpose on the pavement."

On pleasant afternoons the Pease family, who did not own their own carriage, often hired a Victoria and drove along the river in Fairmount Park.[29] On the drive through the Park they would have encountered private coaches with coats of arms emblazoned on their doors to identify the owners.[30]

FOR THOSE WHO lacked coats of arms, Rittenhouse Square continued to provide a somewhat less pleasant reminder—even to small children—of the pervasiveness of snobbery in Philadelphia. But when Theodore Roosevelt stayed on the Square in March 1913, "children of wealthy families, romping in Rittenhouse Square were drawn up at attention when the Colonel passed," a newspaper reported.[31] The following day, when Roosevelt again passed through the Square, roller-skating, marbles, and all other games were abandoned as children ran to get a look at the former president. Roosevelt cheerfully waved at the impressively large group of children.[32] The former president's presence confirmed an impression that was already widespread: Rittenhouse Square had not merely survived the industrialization of Philadelphia; it had established itself as the ultimate upper-class address not just in Philadelphia but in any American city.

Turning Point

[1913–1915]

Dr. J. William White, chairman of physical culture (that is, athletics) at the University of Pennsylvania, was an inveterate social creature who was not afraid to push the boundaries of social convention. White was known for what his friend and biographer Agnes Repplier called his "unaccommodating spirit" and his love of a uniform—two penchants that collided in 1880 when White, who was surgeon of the First City Troop, showed up at a Troop dinner in full troop regalia, rather than the surgeon's customary white trousers and blue frock coat. An objection to Dr. White's uniform by a "brash trooper" led to a challenge and a duel with pistols.

Most accounts place the duel on the Maryland-Delaware border, and some embellish the story with a caterer and champagne.[1] White claimed to have shot into the air, while his adversary claimed to have shot and missed. In any case, White won the battle, if not the duel: From that date on, he wore the "full regalia" of the First City Troop as he had wished.[2]

White's wedding in 1888 to Lettie Disston similarly caused a sensation in Philadelphia because the bride had divorced Henry Disston, a prominent member of Philadelphia society, at a time when divorce was considered scandalous.[3] Yet White's own status as a Philadelphia icon was ensured when his friend Thomas Eakins portrayed him performing surgery in the famous 1889 painting *The Agnew Clinic* (Figure 6.1).

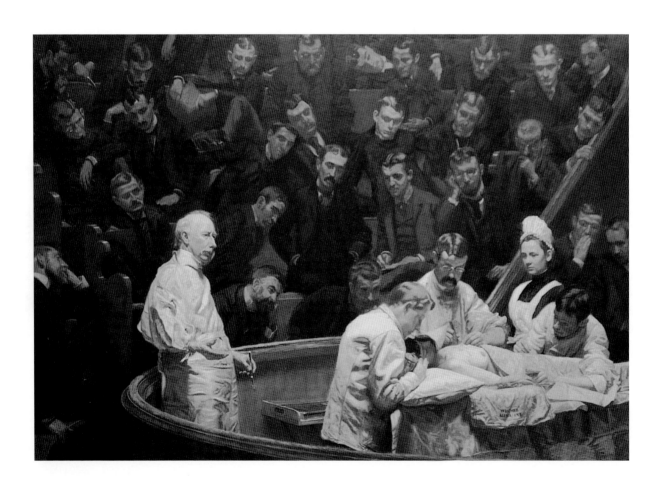

The Whites entertained numerous celebrities in what Henry James referred to as "the cosy little house on Rittenhouse Square"—specifically, 1810 South Rittenhouse Square.[4] When James visited Philadelphia in January 1904 to lecture on Balzac, White was James's host at the Rittenhouse Club, and from that time the two men became good friends. John Singer Sargent was another close friend who spent a month with the Whites in 1903 while painting Mrs. White's portrait. When Sir Arthur Conan Doyle visited White, his enthusiastic host took him to a Penn-Princeton football game. When Theodore Roosevelt visited Philadelphia in 1913, he did so as White's guest.

Like many wealthy Americans after 1890, the Whites developed the practice of touring across Europe, staying at rambling hotels such the Grand Hotel Victoria on the shore of Lake Como, where the Whites stayed in the summer of 1909. Their companions there included his close Philadelphia friend and colleague Dr. Edward Martin. In August they were joined by Martin's sister-in-law, Elizabeth Martin; her invalid husband, Willis; and their daughters.

This was a fortuitous meeting, if in an unlikely locale, of two people who were ideally suited to take on the task of improving Rittenhouse Square. White had recently retired from surgery and had just been appointed to the Fairmount Park Commission. His character, energy, ability, and resolution made him a "valuable . . . colleague and dauntless . . . opponent," as Agnes Repplier put it.[5] Elizabeth Martin, for her part, was a well-connected member of Philadelphia's Price family and an organizer of many social and cultural events.[6] She was, says her biographer,

a unique personality and ardent soul, who fought for others' welfare without pausing to measure her own imperfections or handicaps or fatigues; only seeing her chance to go to the rescue and to annex any who could help in that rescue. A leader, not so much born as disciplined because of circumstances, into giving of herself, and so showing others how to give with her.[7]

At some point in the course of their sojourn at the Grand Hotel Victoria, Bill White and Elizabeth Martin found themselves comparing the beautiful urban parks of Europe to what Repplier called "the dear familiar shabbiness" of their own Rittenhouse Square.[8]

In contrast to the well-manicured beauty of European parks, they lamented, many of Rittenhouse Square's trees had died and others had been topped off. No new planting had been done in years, and "concrete dominated everything." Then and there, William White and Elizabeth Martin resolved to form an organization to improve Rittenhouse Square.[9]

More than three years passed before White and Martin convened a meeting to form the Rittenhouse Square Improvement Association—the first organization with a mandate to improve Rittenhouse Square. On February 19, 1913, some eighty neighbors gathered at the home of Miss Charlotte Siter at 241 South Eighteenth Street (now the site of the Barclay Hotel).[10] As the neighbors discussed the Square and looked toward it through Miss Siter's parlor window, they saw what struck them as a sorry sight.

Of the 144 trees on the Square, between 86 and 114 were dead or dying, and 38 others were in poor condition. Some 70 shrubs were "mostly alive, but not contributing to the beauty of the Square." The Square was unfenced, with a center flagpole and a trash pit in the southeast corner. "It is doubtful," the group agreed in its subsequent report, "that, whether, during the two hundred and twenty or two hundred and thirty years since the dedication of the Square by Penn, it has ever been in a relatively more unkempt and unattractive condition than it is in at present."[11] (To be sure, none of those present had seen the Square in its clay pit days.)

Speakers in Siter's parlor that night included the heads of three city agencies—the Bureau of City Property (which had authority for maintaining Philadelphia's squares), Public Works, and the Bureau of the City Forester. They offered to replant the grass and improve tree pruning within the limits of their budgets.

But the evening's most inspiring vision was provided by Elizabeth Martin, who astutely perceived that one picture is worth a thousand words. With the help of her neighbor Howard Pancoast, who set up a complicated slide mechanism, Martin showed beautiful colored lantern slides she had taken at Parc Monceau in Paris with the aid of the Parisian landscape architect Jacques Gréber. She followed these pictures with slides of Rittenhouse Square. The audience gasped at the contrast.

Martin's choice of Parc Monceau as a model was not entirely fair, since it bore little resemblance to Rittenhouse Square. Then as now, Parc Monceau was three times the size of Rittenhouse Square and contained small lakes, waterfalls, and landscape follies. But the two parks were similar in terms of their elegant surrounding streets and large mansions. What Elizabeth Martin perceived there above all was a well-maintained park placed like a jewel at the center of its neighborhood, and she imagined Rittenhouse Square as the centerpiece of her own community.

It was, she declared, "indeed most lamentable that Rittenhouse Square has been permitted to remain uncared for." She insisted that the Square could be made beautiful by "judicious expenditure of no very great sum."

(A newspaper report the next day was headlined: "Neighborhood Residents Plan to Spend Large Sums to Beautify Breathing Space in Important Residential Section of City." That headline proved more accurate than Mrs. Martin's optimistic forecast.)

This restoration project was consistent with the City Beautiful Movement, a nationwide reform crusade to uplift urban life through large-scale neoclassical renovations. In Philadelphia the movement would find its greatest expression within a few years in the development of the Benjamin Franklin Parkway under the influence of the civic leader Eli Kirk Price II (Elizabeth Martin's brother) and two French architects, Jacques Gréber and Paul Cret, the latter of whom was at the meeting at Charlotte Siter's that night.

Before the group broke up that evening, Paul Cret and Dr. J. Oglesby Paul of the Tree Commission were given a contract to design a landscape. In addition, a committee was selected to draw up a document forming an association dedicated to improving Rittenhouse Square.[12] White was elected president, even though, as Agnes Repplier observed, "It would have been hard to find a man, in or out of town, who knew less about landscape gardening than did Dr. White."[13] It was not so much White's aesthetic expertise as his commitment to public health that informed his enthusiasm for this project: At this time, he was head of the Tree Committee of the Fairmount Park Commission and often lectured on the benefits of street trees to public health.

The new committee issued a circular the following month soliciting memberships and ideas from two groups that would benefit from an improved Square: people who used the Square and landlords whose property values might rise as a result of the improvement. The circular articulated the committee's keen awareness of the Square's function as a public place and as an asset for the entire city, as well as for the Square's immediate vicinity. The annual membership dues were set low ($2.00) in the hope that several individuals within families—especially women and older children—would join.[14]

The Rittenhouse Square Improvement Association drew up its founding charter that November.[15] At the first meeting, White reported that he had raised $30,000 for the Improvement Association's first landscaping project. Within a year the new association would transform the Square into essentially the landscape that Philadelphians know and use to this day.

THE GROUP'S SELECTION of Paul Cret (Figure 6.2) as the Rittenhouse Square architect was a natural choice. Cret had been born and educated in France but came to the United States in 1903 to teach design at the University of Pennsylvania's School of Architecture. His first major American commission, the Organization of American States building in Washington, D.C., in 1907, proved a breakthrough that led to many war memorials, civic buildings, courthouses, and other solid, official structures. Cret was also actively involved in Philadelphia's social scene and its arts community. And, of course, Paris, where Cret had spent his formative years, was the favorite model for the denizens of Rittenhouse Square.

By July 1913—just five months after the initial meeting—Cret's design for the Square was in its final form. Given the approval process—a complicated one even then —five months was remarkably fast work for a city project. The process began with the Rittenhouse Square Improvement Association, which paid the bills for the renovation. Then the proposal went to the Art Jury of Fairmount Park (happily expedited by the membership of Paul Cret and Eli Kirk Price II, the latter the brother of Elizabeth Martin). Finally it had to be approved by the Bureau of City Property.

The landscape Cret designed is basically what we see today: Diagonal crosswalks divided broad sections of grass, which surrounded a slightly elevated central oval terrace enclosed by a limestone balustrade. Each section was anchored by a site for sculpture. Each corner entrance repeated the limestone balustrade and classical urns, with variations at each corner (Figure 6.3).

Cret's system of walkways lent the Square a mazelike quality, creating the illusion of an area larger than the Square's actual 6.2 acres. (Years later the

urbanologist Jane Jacobs quoted a woman living beside the Square who said, "I've used it almost every day for fifteen years, but the other night I tried to draw a plan of it from memory and couldn't. It was too complicated for me.")[16] A diagram shows that this complexity is an illusion created by subtle visual changes and by the choices a walker makes in the course of passing through the Square.

Cret imagined that the central area would be bordered with gravel, providing a playground for little children like the one under the trees of the Jardin des Tuileries in Paris. The reflecting pool, similar to the lagoon in the Luxembourg Gardens in Paris, was conceived by Cret as a place for children to sail their boats. At its center stood a classical mask of Neptune in his seaweed gardens, surrounded by water creatures, all fashioned in colored handmade tile. The whimsical turquoise-and-yellow turtle-and-seaweed design of the tiles backing the fountain underscored Cret's idea of the Square as a place for children to play.

(The colored tiles vanished within a year when Cret returned to France as a soldier in the World War and some unknown official—possibly William White or Eli Kirk Price—had them replaced with plain blue tile.[17] The pebble areas too were replaced eventually by concrete, because children threw the pebbles into the reflecting pool, stopping the drains and causing floods.)

Once the Square's architectural skeleton was established, the next challenge was the greening of the Square. Women like Elizabeth Martin, her sister-in-law Evelyn Price, and Mrs. Charles Cresswell selected the plants and supervised all the planting. In the process, Elizabeth Martin's daughter Marion Martin Rivinus observed in her diary, "Tons of fresh earth, fertilizer and lime have been dumped on the Square. Thousands of flowering plants and shrubs are being set out and several hundred trees of the evergreen variety ordered and prepared for." This was the most menial sort of grunt work, but Marian Rivinus added, "They had a glorious time doing it."[18]

Barely a year after the first organizational meeting at Charlotte Siter's house, new walks, shrubs, and flowerbeds were in place. The central plaza with balustrade and reflecting pool had been constructed according to Cret's design. Antoine-Louis Barye's 1893 sculpture *Lion Crushing a Serpent* had been moved from the north lawn and placed opposite the reflecting pool, and trees had been trimmed, cut down, or transplanted.

There was much left to do, however. The corner entrances were not finished, and the hedge needed time to grow.

Nevertheless, Elizabeth Martin had her "Parc Monceau" jewel. Not until her vision was firmly in place did it become apparent that the Square and its surroundings were heading in different directions. A Parisian-like neighborhood of beaux arts mansions around the Square was not to be. A sea change in the history of Rittenhouse Square was about to take place.

As in the 1850s, when onlookers had watched the Scott mansion being built, another generation of observers gathered in Rittenhouse Square on February 24, 1913, to watch the wrecking balls crash into Anna Scott's Egyptian-style ballroom on the south side of the Square. As they watched, the mansion's mahogany ceilings, ten-foot-tall fireplaces, and massive carved walnut staircase came crashing down into a pile of rubble.[19] Where the Scott family had lived alone, forty luxury apartments (with quarters for domestic help on the top two floors) would rise.

Samuel Price Wetherill, the new apartment building's prime mover, was no nouveau riche Philadelphian; on the contrary, he was a descendant of Samuel Wetherill, who in colonial days had attended the Free Quaker Meeting House along with Betsy Ross. Wetherill's decision to build his own mansion on South Eighteenth Street in 1906 had marked the final acceptance of Rittenhouse Square by the highest social milieu of Old Philadelphians.[20]

Like James Harper nearly a century before him, Wetherill invested in his new neighborhood and, in the process, changed the look of Rittenhouse Square by setting a pattern for the future. But in 1913 the cost of erecting an apartment building was beyond the means of any individual. Wetherill acquired the Scott property through a syndicate of investors. From that point on, development on the Square would be driven not by individuals but by trusts, corporations, and real estate syndicates (Figure 6.4).[21]

Soon after the Scott mansion came down, directly across the Square on Walnut Street, the old Powel/Brown house awaited the wrecking ball. It would make way in 1917 for the Wellington, a thin slice of a building that would become a hotel (Figure 6.5).[22]

The beaux arts style of Wetherill's apartment building at 1830 South Rittenhouse Square reflected Paul Cret's design for the Square, but this building was incongruous in its surroundings. The nineteen-floor shaft of the solitary building towered startlingly 255 feet above its surrounding four-story skyline. A shadow had indeed fallen across the Square—a harbinger of things to come.

ON A VISIT to Paris, two of the Square's grandes dames—Mrs. G. Gordon Meade Large, granddaughter of the Civil War general, and Mrs. Theodore Cramp—had been enchanted by the Flower Market at

■ FIGURE 6.4 (LEFT) *The first high-rise apartment, at 1830 Rittenhouse Square, built in the beaux arts style, showing the scale of the surrounding buildings, circa 1920.*

■ FIGURE 6.5 (RIGHT) *The Wellington, at Nineteenth and Walnut streets, was the second high-rise and the first hotel on the Square. It is shown here about 1920.*
(Temple University Libraries, Urban Archives, Philadelphia, Pennsylvania.)

the Place de la Madeleine. Much like Elizabeth Martin and William White at Lake Como a few years earlier, Mrs. Large and the Cramps sat on a bench in Paris together and wondered, "Why should one not have at home the delights one finds abroad?"[23] Back in Philadelphia, their ingenious idea was to celebrate the completion of the newly landscaped Square with an event to aid children's charities.[24]

The Rittenhouse Flower Market, which opened on May 20, 1914, was a memorable event in the history of Philadelphia's social establishment—one of those rare occasions when "everyone who was anyone" really was there. Mrs. Alexander Cassatt, widow of the Pennsylvania Railroad president, and herself president of Emergency Aid of Pennsylvania, appeared in "a becoming hat with handsome black plumes."[25] The second wife of Edward T. Stotesbury, the J. P. Morgan partner as well as Philadelphia's leading banker, delighted society photographers with her "dainty white gown and rose-wreathed hat."[26] At her home on Walnut Street, Mrs. Stotesbury served lunch on small tables to twenty-four Boy Scouts who had volunteered to act as guides and porters for ladies at the fair (Figure 6.6).

To the strains of the Municipal Band, Bill and Lettie White strolled arm in arm through the "Paris in Miniature" that had been constructed on the Square. At the designated time, the Whites escorted Mayor and Mrs. Rudolph Blankenburg and their party under the red-and-white-striped awnings of the booths to the tent where Elizabeth and Willis Martin entertained them at tea. On the south end of the Square, which was roped off as a "race track," Mary Elizabeth Altemus gave rides in her wagon, which was drawn by her pet goat, which she brought to town from Falls of Schuylkill (later East Falls).[27]

Consistent with the prevailing concept of the Square as a haven for children, the event generated $1,250 each for Children's Hospital, the Hope Day Nursery, and the Rittenhouse Square Improvement Association, which in turn earmarked its share for installation of the lampposts that Paul Cret had designed.

The Flower Market has continued to be an annual event on the Square until the present day.

Unknown to the reporters who breathlessly followed these Philadelphia social luminaries that day, this first Flower Market represented a farewell of sorts to a passing world. Within months, the France that Philadelphia's upper class had sought to emulate was struggling for survival against a German invasion. Paul Cret himself returned to France to fight for his native land. But unlike the shadows cast by Samuel Wetherill's first high-rise, these shadows were not yet apparent. America would not formally enter the World War for three more years, and until then life on the Square continued as before.

THE SQUARE'S OPULENT ERA reached its pinnacle on April 28, 1915, when seventeen-year-old Cordelia Biddle, whose governess once walked her to the Square to play as a child, married the North Carolina tobacco heir Angier Buchanan Duke. By the time the bride arrived at the Church of the Holy Trinity, hundreds of guests and spectators had gathered on the Square, choking traffic to such an extent that even the trolleys were forced to stop. More than a thousand people crowded into Holy Trinity for the vows; twenty-two hundred attended the reception; twenty mounted police officers were required to restrain the onlookers who filled the Square; and the rail yards were clogged with the private rail cars of the Duke family and their guests.[28]

The Square would never again present such a supremely confident profile to the world. Even as the wedding guests bestowed their extravagant gifts—capped by a half-inch sapphire from E. T. Stotesbury—unseen factors were conspiring against the Square. The downtown business area was encroaching on nearby residential streets. The motorcar, like the railroad before it, was encouraging wealthy Philadelphians to flee to the suburbs. And the whole concept of extravagant living itself was being challenged by the new federal income tax, authorized by constitutional amendment in 1913. Increasingly, affluent Philadelphians would have to choose between town and country, and the Square would need to fight for their loyalty in order to survive. Like Cordelia's marriage, the gilded era would not last.

Skyline

[1915–1945]

THE DAY AFTER Cordelia Biddle's wedding, as if to demonstrate that nothing had changed, Cordelia's eccentric father, Anthony J. Drexel Biddle, expropriated the Square for another mass quasi-public event. Major Biddle, as he was called, was a soldier and dilettante boxer whose YMCA-style Bible classes at the Church of the Holy Trinity offered a combination of athleticism and piety that many young people found very appealing.[1] On April 29, 1915, more than six hundred members of Biddle's Athletic Christianity Bible classes—including three bishops, two hundred ministers, and visitors from four foreign countries—marched behind two bands around the Square, singing "Onward Christian Soldiers" as a show of solidarity with the British and French troops already fighting in Europe.[2]

But in fact a great deal had changed for Rittenhouse Square. The Square had found a new function as a setting for public events, but a freshly planted and newly designed Square was less welcoming to the unruly gangs of children who used to run in the old unkempt Square.

The chief of the Bureau of City Property made the rules for the Square, and now there were plenty of them.[3] "Keep off the grass" was one, and it was enforced not only by signs but also by angle irons and wire cord railings placed around the grass plots.

The Square's central portion was reserved for women and children. Roller-skating was permitted only by boys up to age ten and girls up to fourteen. In the "Great Chalk War of 1915," children's right to scribble on sidewalks was questioned.[4]

That same year, the Bureau of City Property relinquished responsibility for the four Philadelphia squares to the Fairmount Park Commission. This shift caused considerable bureaucratic confusion in the ensuing years among the several groups involved with the Square. The Improvement Association retained jurisdiction over planting and shared supervision of the Square's employees with the Park Commission. The Improvement Association continued to finance the payroll, including Christmas presents for employees and, later, wage taxes. Until 1918, it also hired two extra men to assist the three men authorized by the commission. And it paid Billy McLean, a retired prizefighter who served as the Square's watchman and custodian, into the 1920s, when he was past ninety.[5]

With America's entry into World War I in April 1917, work on the Square stalled as its supporters diverted their energies to the war effort. A. J. Drexel Biddle's Bible Class was trained for combat and enlisted in the army as a unit.

Paul Cret was in France from 1914, first as a *poilu* in the trenches and ultimately as an interpreter on the staff of the U.S. commander, General John J. Pershing. But Rittenhouse Square was never far from his thoughts. Early in the war Cret sent back sketches he had made on thin scraps of paper with suggestions for sculpture to be placed on the back of the fountain. This proposal was being discussed by the Rittenhouse Square Improvement Association at the time but was never implemented.[6] In a 1917 letter to Cret in Paris, J. H. Dulles—the owner of Enfield Tiles, which executed the reflecting pool's mural—complained of the difficulty of keeping business going amid the focus on wartime activities. He remarked that the Rittenhouse Square Committee was considering "doing something more there" but added that they would probably wait until Cret's return from France. Cret would not come back until 1919—a year after the war ended—and when he returned, he was partially deaf from the sounds of exploding shells.

ONCE THE WAR was over, the Square's prewar transformation into a public garden inevitably focused attention on the need for decorative elements. Before the war, the only sculpture on the Square was Bayre's *Lion Crushing a Serpent*, first installed in 1893 and relocated during Paul Cret's 1913 renovations. And the process for adding sculpture to the Square had become as complicated as the administration of the Square itself.

Four organizations were involved in overseeing statuary. The Rittenhouse Square Improvement Association was most immediately concerned, but so was the Fairmount Park Commission, since the Square was technically within the Park's jurisdiction. The Fairmount Park Art Association was a nonprofit corporation founded in 1871 by the banker Anthony J. Drexel. Its mission was to purchase works of art for public spaces. This was accomplished through member subscriptions. Toward that end the association purchased and donated art for the city, including sculptures for Rittenhouse Square.

Then there was the city's Art Jury, founded in 1907, which consisted of eight members, appointed by the mayor, who exercised final approval over the city's acquisition of art and its placement.[7]

On paper, this maze of groups seemed a recipe for inertia, as the fate of Paul Manship's fountain statue *The Duck Girl* would seem to suggest. *The Duck Girl* was first exhibited in 1914 at the Pennsylvania Academy of the Fine Arts and soon after was recommended for purchase by the Fairmount Park Art Association's

Committee of Works of Art. But it subsequently encountered artistic grumblings and logistical objections.

"The face looks nowhere and is like a study of a cast," remarked trustee George Morris, who perhaps took his job a little too seriously, at one meeting in 1914. "The movement of legs indicates a walk while the garment shows much motion not caused by wind because hair is quiet. A duck striving so hard would require muscular force to hold. I feel the statue has not been properly studied from life or the artist is unfamiliar with the subject."[8]

To be sure, Morris voted to purchase the statue despite his qualms. But *The Duck Girl* went unappreciated for years. It was first placed in Cloverly Park in Germantown in 1916; ten years later, in 1926, it was displayed temporarily at an Art Alliance exhibit in the Square before being returned to Cloverly Park. When it was vandalized there in the 1940s, it was moved to a Fairmount Park warehouse. It did not make its debut in Rittenhouse Square's reflecting pool until 1960, and even then it was initially placed there only temporarily, until a more suitable location could be found.

Yet in practice most of these groups had overlapping members and were dominated by the Price family and Edward T. Stotesbury, both intimately connected to Rittenhouse Square and adept at working the system. The peripatetic lawyer and civic leader Eli Kirk Price II—Elizabeth Martin's brother—was simultaneously president of the Art Museum, vice president of the Fairmount Park Commission, and a trustee of the Fairmount Park Art Association; as the grandson and namesake of the park's creator (in 1854), Price's influence was virtually hereditary.

Stotesbury, for his part, was the senior partner of the Drexel bank—Philadelphia's most important—and president of the Art Jury since its inception in 1907. He was also president of the Fairmount Park Art Association in 1915 when the bronze figure of a tethered goat, sculpted by the Philadelphian Albert Laessle, first came to his board's attention.[9] The subsequent bureaucratic odyssey of the Square's now-legendary *Billy* offers a good example of how urban progress operated at that time.

The story began in the spring of 1915 when Eli Kirk Price II took a fancy to a small bronze billy goat sculpture, possibly because of its similarity to his own personality and appearance. Many of Price's contemporaries recognized the likeness. "No one who remembers Eli's taut slight figure, his little beard and his lashing glance can see *Billy* without thinking of him," one observer noted (Figure 7.1).[10]

At a meeting of the Fairmount Park Art Association's trustees on April 9, 1915, a member proposed that the association purchase Laessle's bronze goat for the Square, and Eli Kirk Price II immediately seconded the motion. The sum of $800 was allotted. But before the goat could be purchased, the proposal was referred to the association's Committee on Works of Art, which concluded that

■ FIGURE 7.1 *Eli Kirk Price II, who was often compared in looks and personality to* Billy the Goat, *his "anonymous" gift to the Square.*
(*Bust of Eli Kirk Price*, Einar Jonsson. Courtesy of the Philadelphia Museum of Art: gift of Evelyn Taylor Price, 1933.)

the sculpture was too small for any available site and sent the artist a $25 honorarium for his trouble.[11]

But that was hardly the end of the story. The supremely self-confident Eli Kirk Price II was infamous for ignoring the opinions of fellow members of his numerous civic boards. His style was to reach a firm conclusion in his own mind, then quietly bide his time "until everyone else got their arguments all out of their system," as his niece Marion Martin Rivinus put it. At that point he would subtly push, "always in the direction of his clear goal"—in this case, installation of *Billy* in Rittenhouse Square.[12]

A few years later, when everyone else had forgotten about *Billy*, an anonymous patron of the arts—generally believed to be Eli Kirk Price II himself—bought the statue and donated it to the city. In 1920, five years after that first meeting, the sculpture was finally installed in the Square, just as Eli Kirk Price had intended all along.

At first *Billy* was not a critical success. "The animal is not only an insult to the intelligence of art lovers," the *Public Ledger* claimed; it "is positively vulgar." The article facetiously suggested moving the sculpture to the Park Commission meeting room, "so they could enjoy the pleasure of such high-grade company in repose and quiet."[13]

But the children who played in the Square liked *Billy* better than the critics did, and by 1924 the press had changed its tune. *Billy*, wrote one paper, had been in the Square "for several seasons, but age has not withered nor custom staled him for his young devotees." Another paper called *Billy* a "charming and welcome innovation of recent years." Still another article proclaimed, "The children who frequent this square can never forego a ride on his back, and the little hands clasping his horns have entirely rubbed the patina from the bronze, so that the points appear to be tipped with gold."[14]

Soon Billy McLean, the Square's octogenarian park guard, took to spreading a myth among children who played there: Each night at midnight, when the

Square was deserted, Billy the goat would come off his perch and graze on the grass. When Eli Kirk Price II died in 1933 at his home at 1709 Walnut Street, it was clear that his presence would remain on the Square in perpetuity in the person of the little bronze goat.

EVEN THE PRICE FAMILY could not forestall the changes on Rittenhouse Square's periphery after World War I. Indeed, one of the greatest achievements of Eli Kirk Price II—the opening of the Benjamin Franklin Parkway in 1919—played a part in hastening those changes. On his various civic boards, Price had worked incessantly to pump new life into downtown Philadelphia with a broad, dramatic, diagonal boulevard that would slice across the heart of William Penn's 236-year-old grid plan and provide a showcase for Philadelphia's newest cultural institutions. The two Frenchmen who designed the Parkway—Paul Cret and Jacques Gréber—modeled the Parkway after the Champs-Elysées in their native Paris in the hope that the Parkway would do for Philadelphia what the Champs-Elysées had done for Paris: remind the world that cities are desirable not merely as places to work but as places to enjoy as well. Yet as an unintended side effect, the Parkway became one more factor—along with suburban railroads, the motorcar, and the opening of Roosevelt Boulevard—facilitating the commute to Germantown and Chestnut Hill and thus further encouraging the exodus of families from the city.[15]

As the families left the Rittenhouse Square neighborhood, the schools followed. Declining enrollment forced the DeLancey School to be merged into Episcopal Academy in 1915; but even so, Episcopal Academy could not sustain enrollment in the city and moved to Overbrook in 1921.[16] The Episcopal boys who had played, skated, and taunted each other were now gone from the Square.

The Agnes Irwin School for girls remained on Delancey Place a decade longer, but by 1926 more than half of its senior class commuted from the suburbs, either by the Paoli Local or "in little roadsters or coupes with rumble seats, twisting and turning through Fairmount Park and waving gaily to the traffic guards," as a school history put it. By 1933 the Agnes Irwin School departed for the Main Line suburbs as well. "Never again at recess would they slip to the corner to buy an apple from 'good old Dominic' or a gardenia for ten cents including pins," lamented a school history written in 1960. "Nor in the afternoons would they be able to window-shop, or stroll through Rittenhouse Square."[17]

Absent these students, the Square would no longer serve as the sort of playground it had been. As families moved out, businesses moved in, deepening the gloom of the families that remained. "Today the glory of Walnut Street is no more," mourned George Pepper, who so fondly remembered his childhood on the Square in the 1870s. "As I look at the vacant city lots now used as parking places it gives me a bit of a pang to recall the fine old mansions which once stood there. The old saying that in three generations an American family goes from shirt sleeves to shirt sleeves might be supplemented by the lament that in a like period many historic homes have gone from dust to dust."[18]

As early as 1916, one newspaper observed, "From the Delaware to the Schuylkill, there is scarcely a block on Chestnut Street that is not wholly or partly—and usually wholly—occupied by business. As for the dwelling houses that remain in what used to be called the *West End*, it is common to forecast that they will all lose their residential status in the next few years and fall into the hands of trade."[19] This was a dire prediction indeed for what at that point was still Philadelphia's most prestigious residential neighborhood.

By the 1920s more than one hundred thousand automobiles were counted in the city, where only five hundred had operated in 1905.[20] When all those motorcars were not ferrying Philadelphians to and from the suburbs, they needed parking places in the city, and lots began to spring up around the Square to accommodate them. At Eighteenth and Walnut streets, three mansions were demolished for parking lots, which remained on that southeast corner for twenty years. Another victim of this scourge was the former home of the Pennsylvania Railroad president Edgar Thomson at Eighteenth and Spruce streets, occupied by his widow until her death in 1912.[21] A collateral victim of that particular demolition was a cherished ancient elm tree whose branches spread all the way across Eighteenth Street; despite local efforts to raise money to move this huge tree, it was cut down and sold for firewood.[22]

The age of large mansions around the Square ended in the 1920s because few people could afford them any more—and those few who could were inclined to flee an increasingly commercial neighborhood for bucolic and increasingly accessible suburbs. But during this period, visionary real estate developers perceived a new and far more profitable constituency for the Square.

Samuel Wetherill, who had ushered in the Square's apartment era in 1913 with his building at 1830 South Rittenhouse Square, resisted the postwar temptation to turn vacant mansions into parking lots for a quick profit. The rich may have departed, but the cachet of a Rittenhouse Square address remained, not just for the very wealthy, but also for the merely affluent, especially now that more affordable flats were available there.

Thus out of the ruins of bygone mansions, the age of apartment living—that is, the age of density—arrived on Rittenhouse Square. When the war ended in 1918, the Square numbered only two high-rise apartment buildings: Wetherill's, on the south side of Rittenhouse Square, at number 1830; and the Wellington, at Nineteenth and Walnut streets. But during the 1920s, five more arose in rapid succession. In these luxurious buildings an affluent professional man and his family could fancy themselves members of the elite for a fraction of the upkeep on a mansion; and a landlord could draw rents from two or three dozen families in a space previously occupied by only one. Some of the Square's mansions had stood empty for years, but the new high-rises filled rapidly.

Across Nineteenth Street from Samuel Wetherill's beaux arts high-rise, on the corner of South Rittenhouse Square, an eighteen-story luxury apartment building opened in 1924 where the Drexel mansion had previously stood.[23] This "1900

South Rittenhouse Square," as it was called, offered two units per floor, which effectively meant that thirty-six apartments replaced a single dwelling. It was followed in 1927 on the west side of the Square by the Chateau Crillon, noted for its signature roof designed by Horace Trumbauer; and by the Rittenhouse Plaza on Walnut Street, a Spanish art deco building, complete with Moorish motif tiles and arches on its top floors, wrought iron gates and window screens in the courtyard, and a Spanish name, "Plaza," for its location on a park. Yet another apartment building—a neat, prim redbrick high-rise in a neo-Georgian style—opened at 225 South Eighteenth Street in 1928. The fifth multistory building rose on the northeast corner of Eighteenth and Walnut streets.

Perhaps the most dramatic departure from the old Rittenhouse Square was the ultramodern Pennsylvania Athletic Club, a state-of-the-art building on Eighteenth Street that offered 350 bedrooms (with baths) as well as restaurants, a swimming pool, tennis courts, a bowling alley, and health club facilities (including separate facilities and dining room for ladies).

Some of the new residents of these buildings were older people from established families who already lived in the area. John and Lavinia Lowry moved from 126 South Nineteenth Street (north of the Square) to 1900 South Rittenhouse Square "because of the view," said their granddaughter. They chose a second-floor apartment so that Lavinia, who was not well, would be able to look out on the people on the Square. Their granddaughter, who visited from Haverford as a child, remembered a big apartment that "went back very far. It had a nice living room on the front with this lovely view. . . . They had oriental rugs and old furniture."[24]

The Square's newly affluent class was perhaps epitomized by Michael Francis Doyle and his wife, Nancy, who lived in splendor on the top floor of 1900 South Rittenhouse Square. Doyle moved to Rittenhouse Square from South Philadelphia; his path to the Square derived not from old family money but from his Penn law degree and his international law practice, which required him to spend much of his time abroad, beyond the Square's earlier close-knit social circle.[25]

With their Irish background, the Doyles would feel a special affinity for this location: On the same property nearly a century earlier, the wives of Irish coal heavers had hung out their wash; and later in the nineteenth century Irish servants had worked for the Drexels and Wanamakers in the mansion on this spot. Like the original Goosetown Irish, the Doyles belonged to St. Patrick's Church on Twentieth Street. (St. Patrick's itself was replaced in 1910 with a new larger church in the Byzantine style, with a grand staircase entrance where the old street-level church had stood.)

As a young man, Doyle himself had worked as an errand boy for Thomas Wanamaker, son of the famous department store magnate John Wanamaker.[26] According to an apocryphal story, Thomas Wanamaker once sent young Michael to the Wanamaker mansion to deliver some jewelry to his wife. When Doyle arrived at the mansion, he was scolded by the butler for coming to the front door (rather than the service entrance on Manning Street) and attempting to approach the mistress of the house directly.[27] Young Doyle supposedly vowed at that moment that one day he would live in that house.[28] And indeed he subsequently bought the mansion and built the apartment house there.

At the Wellington on Walnut Street, the residents included the millionaire coal broker John McFadden and his wife, who were the last occupants of the Powel/Brown home that had been razed in 1917 to make way for the Wellington. In effect this arrangement enabled the McFaddens to keep their view without their previous upkeep.[29] Their magnificent collection of eighteenth-century English paintings, said to be the best in the world at the time, now hung on apartment walls. (Upon his death in 1921, McFadden left his collection to the Philadelphia Museum of Art building that Eli Kirk Price was already planning for the west end of Ben Franklin Parkway.)

Rittenhouse Square's new high-rise apartments now beckoned as well to Eastern European Jewish immigrants who had settled in South Philadelphia at the turn of the century and had subsequently prospered and assimilated. Although

Jewish residents had numbered among the Square's neighbors since the days of the Cohens, Mordecais, and Rosengartens in the nineteenth century, Jews now became a significant presence there, markedly enhancing the Square's new cosmopolitan flavor. The Lit brothers, who lived on Nineteenth Street, were among the founders in 1920 of the Locust Club, the Jewish men's club east of the Square on Locust Street. The motion picture pioneers Jules and Stanley Mastbaum lived on the south side of the Square. Rabbi William H. Fineshriber, spiritual leader of Reform Congregation Keneseth Israel, moved to the Square in the 1920s and remained there long after his retirement in the 1940s. Philip Klein's advertising and public relations agency occupied the ground floor of a town house on the Square's south side, and he and his family lived upstairs. The neighborhood's first Jewish congregation, Temple Beth Zion, held its first services in 1946. By 1954 that congregation occupied the Gothic stone church at Eighteenth and Spruce streets that had previously housed the Brickmakers' Church, which had moved there from Twentieth Street in 1894 (Figure 7.2).[30]

The sociological shift implied in the transition from old-moneyed town houses to new-moneyed apartment buildings was perceptively captured in a work of fiction: *It's Not Done*, a Philadelphia novel published in 1926. According to the book's author, William C. Bullitt, the old-guard protagonist received a note from someone in a high-rise building, complaining about "somebody in your house who takes baths and dresses without drawing the blinds on the third floor":

"Of all the damned impudence!" John's lower jaw crept out until it was overshot. "Is the fellow who wrote this waiting?"

"No, sir, it was just a bellboy from the apartment house."

"Well, what do you think it says, Pullen? Mr. L. Strauss, whoever that may be . . . has the gall to tell me to stop using the bathroom without pulling the blinds! I've bathed in this bathroom since I was four! They've cut off the sun with their damned apartment, and now! Just go

■ FIGURE 7.2 *The new Brickmakers' Methodist Church, built in the Gothic style, arose at Eighteenth and Spruce streets in 1894. It was purchased in 1954 to become the new home of Temple Beth Zion (later Beth Zion–Beth Israel).* (Photograph by Nancy Heinzen.)

over to Mr. L. Strauss, please, Pullen, and tell him from me that he can go to hell."

"Yes, sir."

"And if he has the impertinence to answer you, just tell him that if his cliff dwellers don't like what they see when they have the effrontery to look in my windows they can look the other way, and if they don't like that he can pull down his damned apartment house. I've done what I'm doing now since before it existed, and I'll go on using my house as I see fit."

"Yes, sir. Do you really want me to see him, sir?"

"No, I suppose I'd better get hold of the owners and have him fired."

"I think he owns it, sir."

"Probably! It would be Strauss or Cohen or Levy! By God, I'd like to blow it up! Just having it there has almost ruined the Square."[31]

The Barclay on Eighteenth Street, built as a residential hotel in 1929, became the Square's most fashionable and expensive residence. In due course the Barclay became an enduring symbol of continuity through changing times. Its dining room was famous for Caesar, the imposing maitre d', who knew everyone's favorite dish and drink. The Barclay's hat-check girls, Christine and Peggy, started working in the early 1930s and were still checking hats and coats in their starched aprons more than thirty-five years later—although, as one of them pointed out, "We can hardly be called hat check girls because we don't have checks—we know everyone's coat."[32]

The Barclay was also the last of the Square's first-generation high-rises. Even as fox-trotting debutantes celebrated its gala opening in the Georgian ballroom, the stock market crash that same month set the stage for the Great Depression. With it, the Square's apartment construction boom came to a screeching halt.

In any case, not every home around the Square was replaced by a high-rise. Many townhouses were preserved for at least another generation through conversion into apartments or studios for artists, musicians, and students. The 1920s and 1930s also witnessed a restoration renaissance in the small streets around the Square, such as Panama Street, where Senator George Wharton Pepper had lived as a child.

Other homes around the square were saved from the wrecking ball through conversion to institutional use. After sitting on the market for three years, E. T. Stotesbury's gorgeous ballroom addition on Walnut Street became the home of the Philopatrian Society. The palatial Joseph Harrison home along Eighteenth Street housed the Red Cross and the Emergency Aid before the mansion was pulled down to make way for the Penn Athletic Club. "Physick's Folly" at Nineteenth and Walnut streets was used by the French War Relief committee before it was pulled down to build the Rittenhouse Plaza in 1927. In 1924, Alexander Van Rensselaer bought the Walnut Street properties adjoining his mansion at Eighteenth Street for the Presbyterian Ministers Insurance Fund (it was later known as the Alison Building); when his wife, society's grande dame Sarah Drexel Fell Van Rensselaer, died in 1929, their mansion sat vacant for ten years before the Penn Athletic Club—a victim of the Depression and World War II—moved there from its high-rise a half block down Eighteenth Street.

On the Square's west side, the Fairman Rogers/Alexander Cassatt house, next to the Church of the Holy Trinity, became the offices of the Episcopal Diocese of Philadelphia. The Pancoast/Lippincott house at the corner of Locust Street became home to the Red Cross Society and then the City Institute Library. The Ethical Society, an offshoot of the quasi-religious New York Society for Ethical Culture, moved to the south side of the Square in 1930 when it acquired two adjoining houses there; like the Rittenhouse Club in the nineteenth century, the Ethical Society joined the buildings into a hall for meetings and lectures.

Through all this flux, a few old-guard diehards blithely remained. Mrs. John A. Brown, Jr., continued to serve tea in the grand style, with a liveried butler, at 224 West Rittenhouse Square, her winter residence from the time she married in

1887 until she died in 1941.[33] (After housing the Italian Consulate following her death, the house was torn down in the 1950s to make way for what would become the Dorchester Apartments.)[34] Susan Sturgis wintered in her home on Walnut Street until her death in 1946. Her house would be replaced by the garage at 1845 Walnut Street.

Yet those Philadelphians like George Pepper who mourned the end of the Square's Gilded Age were outnumbered by those who welcomed the high-rises and conversions as a sign of fresh vitality. "The square today presents a studied arrangement of plantings, walks and interesting sculpture which give to it some of the dignity and beauty of the London squares," the *Public Ledger* saw fit to observe in 1932. "And the skyline of Philadelphia itself, seen from the square, has been said by many to be the most beautiful and impressive in America."[35]

ALMOST IMPERCEPTIBLY, a change more subtle than one of bricks and mortar took place on Rittenhouse Square in the 1920s. In many respects the mansion dwellers' lifestyle had imitated that of English manor houses: It was exclusive, smug, self-satisfied, and centered on private gatherings among a small, tight social circle preoccupied with preserving their old ways. Apartment dwellers, by contrast, were more cosmopolitan: They tended to be open, inclusive, curious, adventurous. They tended to be younger as well. As the mansion dwellers moved to the country, the millionaire in the top hat was increasingly replaced as the icon of Rittenhouse Square by the earnest young music student with the violin case. As a consequence, the Rittenhouse Square neighborhood that had only recently symbolized high society now became a center of arts and culture—the sort of "little Bohemia" that had not been seen in Philadelphia since the city's golden age as the "Athens of America" a century earlier.

The first vestige of the transformation occurred in 1911 when Samuel Wetherill's daughter, Christine Wetherill Stevenson, together with Mrs. Eli Kirk Price and Mrs. Otis Skinner, wife of the well-known actor, formed "The Plays and Players," an amateur dramatic group composed mostly of neighborhood residents. The following year, on the 1700 block of Delancey Street, they opened a little 324-seat jewel box of a theater, complete with wall murals by Edith Emerson depicting the legend of Dionysus.[36]

Christine Wetherill Stevenson, then in her thirties, was a creative woman, interested in all the arts: In 1911 she went to Hollywood, where she wrote and produced *Light of Asia*, a film based on the theosophist philosophy that she practiced.[37] The Hollywood Bowl, which she helped to finance, was built to house the "pilgrimage play" that she produced. Christine Stevenson appears to have been inspired by New York's Armory Show of 1913—America's first international exhibition of modern art—and deeply concerned by Europe's Great War that began in 1914. She often held meetings, rehearsals, and philanthropic conferences, and at one such "talk fest"—held in 1915 during a salon at Samuel Wetherill's mansion on Eighteenth Street—the Philadelphia Art Alliance was formed (Figure 7.3).[38]

■ FIGURE 7.3 *Christine Wetherill Stevenson (circa 1913), who founded the first forum for the arts on the Square.* (Courtesy of Philadelphia Art Alliance.)

"If civilizing forces are to be upheld in this period of strife and horror," she explained in a brochure, "American institutions must be proportionately constructive."[39]

Christine Stevenson originally expected the Art Alliance to emphasize theater, but the organization soon turned its focus to the visual arts. In 1917, Samuel Wetherill bought two of James Harper's original houses on the 1800 block of Walnut Street and then sold them to the Art Alliance. Three years later, the Art Alliance acquired a third adjoining property, and all three homes on Walnut were reconfigured into nineteen artists' studios and nine apartments. In 1920 the Art Alliance organized a sculpture exhibit in its rear garden and in Rittenhouse Square, which was repeated biennially until 1942. Paul Cret supervised the arrangements.[40]

Christine Stevenson was only forty-four when she died in 1922. When her father, Samuel Wetherill, died four years later, the Art Alliance bought his mansion on Eighteenth Street, in accordance with the terms of his will. (Wetherill's widow and his son Samuel P. Wetherill, Jr., chose to move into his high-rise, 1830 Rittenhouse Square.) "Not only because of its architectural features, and the desirable location, is the move a happy one," the *Art Alliance Bulletin* noted; "there is the added romance that the Art Alliance is to be sheltered beneath the hospitable roof of its inception."[41] This remarkable institution subsequently provided a cultural showcase with visits and lectures by such luminaries as Leopold Stokowski (himself a nearby resident), Le Corbusier, Frank Lloyd Wright, Gertrude Stein, and Igor Stravinsky. And the Art Alliance remained a family affair: Samuel P. Wetherill, Jr., served as its president from 1926 to 1936.[42]

About the same time, Mary Louise Curtis Bok (daughter of the magazine publishing magnate Cyrus Curtis), who had become interested in the Settlement Music School for culturally deprived children in South Philadelphia, decided to create a separate school to train talented students for professional music careers (Figure 7.4). To this end she purchased two properties on Rittenhouse Square,

■ FIGURE 7.4 *Mary Louise Curtis Bok Zimbalist, pictured on the occasion of her eightieth birthday in 1954. She is seated with Margaret Ormandy.* (Courtesy of the Curtis Institute of Music.)

most notably the George W. Childs Drexel mansion at Eighteenth and Locust streets, former home of Cordelia Biddle's imperious Aunt Mary Drexel. Mrs. Bok's endowment enabled the Curtis Institute of Music to offer free tuition to any student who was accepted, as well as other enticements, such as a Steinway baby grand for every piano student. Consequently, almost from the moment the Institute opened its doors in the fall of 1924, it attracted some of the world's most talented music students and consequently the greatest teachers. (Leopold Stokowski conducted the first rehearsal of the Curtis Orchestra, and many Philadelphia Orchestra musicians became members of the Curtis faculty.)

The opening of Curtis occurred one year after the arrival on the Square of the Philadelphia City Institute, which since its opening in 1855 had sought to improve the lives of disadvantaged young men and women by offering an excellent library, reading room, lectures, and a free night school. For its first sixty-eight years the City Institute was located at Eighteenth and Chestnut streets, but in 1923 it moved into the Pancoast/Lippincott house on the west side of the Square.

With the establishment of these artistic and intellectual anchors—followed in 1934 by Helen Corning Warden's Academy of Vocal Arts—the Rittenhouse Square area took on a character of high culture. Writers, musicians, painters, and art collectors shared their common interests in literary salons and musicales. At Friday and Saturday night parties, "the painters, the Museum people and amateurs of one sort or another mixed in the belief that something exciting was happening," noted one historian.[43]

Leopold Stokowski, conductor of the Philadelphia Orchestra between 1912 and 1936, lived just off the Square (at 1716 Rittenhouse Square Street) and was at the center of some of the salons—a glamorous figure who kept his neighbors gossiping with his golden curls, his "international" accent, and his flamboyant lifestyle, which included two ex-wives and the film actress Greta Garbo.[44] R. Sturgis Ingersoll—lawyer, grandson of Susan Sturgis, and, as president of the Art Museum, the prime mover of the museum's permanent Greek temple, which opened in Fairmount in 1928—held a well-known salon after orchestra concerts at his home on Rittenhouse Square.[45] Theo White described attending one of these salons with Paul and Madame Cret:

> After the concert Cret loaded the three of us into the back seat of the taxi while he sat on the floor at our feet and amused us by blowing into his glove and counting the outstretched fingers of the inflated glove. The taxi took us to the house of Miss Anna Ingersoll in Walnut Street, overlooking Rittenhouse Square. There were a number of people in the charming second-floor drawing room. In one corner sat Leopold Stokowski, conductor of the Orchestra, relaxed in an emotional and physical fatigue.[46]

On the south side of the Square, Stokowski also made appearances at the frequent soirees hosted in the 1940s by Esther and Philip Klein at their South Rittenhouse Square town house. Esther perhaps epitomized the rising nucleus of Jewish audiences and patrons who increasingly nurtured and funded the city's cultural life: Among other things, she was a founder of the Rittenhouse Orchestra volunteers and cohost, with her husband, of *Mr. and Mrs. Breakfast*, a radio show about cultural events broadcast from their home at 1910 South Rittenhouse Square. Esther Klein recounted one intimate dinner party at her home when Stokowski showed up uninvited with an entourage of six young protégés. Living up to her reputation as an exemplary hostess, Mrs. Klein took it in stride and made sure that everyone had a wonderful time.[47]

The downside of this "little Bohemia" during the Prohibition years of the 1920s and the Depression of the 1930s was a general sense of insecurity downtown. Many formerly handsome homes were turned into boardinghouses for an increasingly transient population. Women, reported the *Evening Bulletin* in 1934, were "molested on the streets at night by racketeers who are making speakeasies and gambling joints in the Rittenhouse Square their latest hangout."[48] A safety patrol group calling themselves the Vigilantes blamed a series of holdups and robberies in "the apartment-hotel district" on poor street lighting and an understaffed police force.[49] Only after a dressmaker named Mrs. Parks was cut by a milk bottle thrown in a brawl were plainclothes policemen assigned to the Square.[50]

Still, to at least one observer decades later it seemed as if "a Depression went by and scarcely ruffled the grass."[51] The Rittenhouse Square Improvement Association persisted, albeit with a slightly different cast. Its founder, Elizabeth Price Martin, died in 1932—flags in the city flew at half-mast—and her brother Eli Kirk Price II died the following year. The next generation of the Price family moved permanently to Chestnut Hill in 1935. Yet many Association members remained involved in the Square even after they had moved away. In 1934, with Eli Kirk Price's widow as president, the Improvement Association successfully opposed a proposal to cut a road through the northwest corner of the Square to improve the traffic flow at Nineteenth and Walnut streets. Instead the corners were merely rounded, so cars could turn at the same time as streetcars.[52]

The Improvement Association's other major projects included a plan for a new fence around the Square's perimeter in 1937, to be financed by the city, and new entrances to the Square in 1940, using Paul Cret's plans.[53] (The fence was not erected until 1976.)

The Depression notwithstanding, the Flower Market continued uninterrupted throughout the 1930s. And in 1932, the Clothesline Art Exhibit was added to the chain of annual events on the Square (Figure 7.5). This event began when Samuel Fleisher, a Fairmount Park commissioner, grew interested in a group of

■ Figure 7.5 *The Clothesline Exhibit was founded to promote young student artists who had no place to exhibit their work.* (Temple University Libraries, Urban Archives, Philadelphia, Pennsylvania.)

high school students who called themselves the Art Students League. To encourage them, Fleisher organized an outdoor exhibit, with prizes awarded by jury. He prevailed upon the Fairmount Park Commission to hold it in Rittenhouse Square on the first weekend in June. The students displayed their best works of the past year, fastened to ropes strung from tree to tree, transforming the Square into "Montmartre of Paris."[54] The Art Alliance provided a room in which sales of the exhibited works could be transacted. Some lucky buyers acquired works by students who later became recognized artists. (The show subsequently evolved into an art market for professionals.)

Two more statues were added to the Square in the 1940s. A granite French frog by Cornelia Van Auken Chapin was brought to Philadelphia in 1940 after being exhibited at the World's Fair in New York.[55] In 1947 a sundial by Beatrice Fenton was commissioned by the Flower Market and placed in the Square to honor Evelyn Taylor Price (Mrs. Eli), the Flower Market's former president.

Although children no longer dominated the Square as they had in the days of George Wharton Pepper and Henry Cohen, the available evidence suggests that the Square was still frequented by at least enough children to cause a perpetual maintenance problem. In 1942 the Fairmount Park Commission was urged to institute legal proceedings against people who threw pebbles or debris into the reflecting pool.[56] It was probably Paul Cret himself who instigated this action with a letter to Eli Kirk Price III that reflected Cret's European bias:

> The children at the Square are anything but co-operative, and apparently it is impossible to enforce any decent behavior as would have been done in peace-times, in Paris, or any other city of the Old World. The children deliberately throw handfuls of pebbles and any refuse at hand into the [reflecting] pool—one child carried successive handfuls of pebbles and emptied them in the scum gutter, while its mother stood nearby giggling. When the caretaker expostulated, this mother flew into a

temper and said she was a taxpayer and that the children could do what they wanted.[57]

Replacing the pebbles soon became the only solution, and the center inside the pool's balustrade was paved with asphalt.

BY DECEMBER 1941, America was again at war. In the years that followed, Walnut Street residents often awoke on Sundays to witness a procession of twenty to forty soldiers, sailors, and marines (as well as an occasional woman) on their way to Holy Trinity for services. It was hardly the grand Easter Parade of the Square's Gilded Age, but no less important to those who sought now what the Square had always provided in one way or another: the power of community in restoring the human spirit.

Things We Should Fight For

[1945–1968]

WITH THE END of World War II, America's postwar economy took off just as it had done following the Civil War eighty years earlier. The automobile whisked people out to Americans' presumed suburban dream: a house and lawn on one's own piece of land. Americans still worked downtown, but increasingly they commuted there from somewhere else.

"The old town has become a mere stopping-place for commuters," wrote a Philadelphia architecture critic in 1953, "a place to traffic in and get out of." As for Rittenhouse Square, it was "habited only by sitters in the sun and those melancholy young men who lead dogs on their matutinal walks."[1]

In Philadelphia the newly created City Planning Commission went right to work, with plans to demolish the Pennsylvania Railroad's Broad Street Station. The infamous "Chinese wall" along west Market Street was to be replaced by a maze of boxlike modern high-rise office buildings seated atop a submerged

Suburban Station, so commuters could travel to work and home without even glimpsing the city outside.

Rittenhouse Square had seen better days. Very little had been done since its 1913 remake. Fairmount Park, with some money from the Rittenhouse Square Improvement Association, did its best to maintain the Square, but in any case city parks occupied a low priority in the municipal budget.

Around the Square, buildings were going commercial. The Pennsylvania Athletic Club's high-rise on Eighteenth Street was now an office building occupied by the U.S. Army Signal Corps. (The club itself had moved up Eighteenth Street to the old Van Rensselaer mansion on the corner of Walnut.) Commercial offices had invaded the Wellington on Walnut. The twin-towered Rittenhouse Plaza Apartments on Walnut Street were about to be sold to the Commonwealth of Pennsylvania for offices. No one living on or near Rittenhouse Square could be certain where commercial development would spread from there, but the Square area seemed a likely candidate. To many residents in June 1950, "the Square was doomed to become a commercial center," one of them later recalled.[2]

So in 1950, when a development firm called Underground Garages, Inc., made a proposal to build a parking garage beneath Rittenhouse Square, it might have signaled the beginning of the end of the Square as Philadelphians had known it for the past century. Instead, the garage crisis became the rallying point for a new civic organization and indeed a revived vision of urban life (Figure 8.1).

Like the Rittenhouse Square Improvement Association a generation earlier, a new organization was inspired by a Philadelphian's dismay upon returning from abroad. When Clark Hanna came home from World War II, he was appalled at the condition of his old neighborhood and organized an informal residents' group that pressed the city for improved upkeep of the Square. This group formed the nucleus of a September 1946 meeting at which nearly three hundred neighbors jammed into the Art Alliance to create the Center City Residents Association (CCRA), a formal organization for residents living between Broad Street and the Schuylkill River.[3]

■ FIGURE 8.1 *The 1950
plan for the underground
garage that would
galvanize the residents
into a strong civic
organization.*
(Temple University
Libraries, Urban
Archives, Philadelphia,
Pennsylvania.)

The association's first president was Walter Hudson, resident manager of the Embassy Apartments on Walnut Street.[4] Unlike an earlier generation of neighborhood leaders, Hudson harbored no sentimental attachment to the status quo. Instead he sought to influence the area's inevitable business transition in the direction of arts and culture rather than industry and commerce. One of CCRA's early brochures promoted the notion that "there's more to Center City than Rittenhouse Square."

"One tie that links the whole area," Hudson argued, "is a common interest in the things that are distinctively a part of city life—music, the theater, lectures, the libraries, the museums. Call it culture, for lack of a better word. And, of course, the shops and the general air of activity."[5] This "activity," Hudson contended, allowed Center City "to hold to its personality despite the crumbling of ancient mansions, the steady march of commerce and outward change in the social status of its population."[6]

Still, CCRA galvanized only modest support until the underground garage proposal surfaced. Rumors of the garage first reached Hudson late in May 1950.[7] A week later, at the Embassy, the CCRA board met with the underground garage project's architect and engineer, who explained their plans to build beneath Rittenhouse Square. Alarmed, Hudson called an emergency CCRA meeting with the developers for June 19. In the week leading up to the meeting, Hudson's mail drop at the Embassy was inundated with letters, notes, telegrams, and petitions opposing the proposal.

The opposition centered on several themes: the historic nature of the Square, its role as an urban oasis, and its position as the focal point of a prestigious residential area. Residents who might have been apathetic about other civic issues seemed to arise en masse when the Square's integrity was threatened. Their arguments were framed in the passionate language that similar threats to Rittenhouse Square had evoked in the past.

"It is unthinkable that harm would be done to a place that gives so much pleasure to young and old," wrote one resident, Mae Pease. "Rittenhouse Square is perhaps the best section we have left in Philadelphia," added L. Stauffer Oliver. The garage plan, thundered Lucien Phillips, "is one of the most diabolical schemes ever conceived by a body of Philadelphia citizens and should be fought against with all the means we have at our disposal."[8]

At the appointed meeting on June 19, 1950, five hundred agitated neighbors jostled for seats in the YWCA on Chestnut Street. Hudson opened the meeting by drawing piles of letters and telegrams from his briefcase with both hands and then slapping them on the table with a ceremonious thud. That gesture set the tone for an evening of fiery speeches by George Gordon Meade (heir and namesake of the Civil War hero), Judge L. Stauffer Oliver, Fuery Ellis, and Esther and Philip Klein, some of whom threatened a march on City Hall as well as legal action against the garage developer.[9]

Alan Emlen, the developer's sole representative at the meeting, seemed utterly unprepared for the communal wrath provoked by the garage proposal. He was "an innocent youth, born and raised in the suburbs, who may have never even seen Rittenhouse Square," in the view of Marion Rivinus, who represented the Rittenhouse Square Improvement Association at the meeting.[10]

Emlen (who actually lived in Chestnut Hill) later publicly dismissed the neighbors' speeches as "fatuous arguments" put forth by "allegedly prominent citizens." The meeting itself, he complained, was a "hoedown" that "hooted and hollered the plan out of existence."[11] Clark Hanna saw it differently, describing an "orderly and unanimous vote . . . after ample opportunity for all views to be presented."[12] Two days after the meeting, on June 21, the Committee on City Property announced that the proposal was dead and that it would not be submitted to City Council.

The effect of this victory over commercial and political interests by the Center City Residents Association—which was, after all, a volunteer organization with no legal standing—left members and residents euphoric about their collective effectiveness. "The fight is over!" marveled Adelaide Sheble in a typical congratulatory letter to Hudson. "The victory is won!" In its first serious challenge, CCRA had established itself as a force to be reckoned with.

But in fact the fight was hardly over. Little more than a year later, in October 1951, Hudson heard another rumor that turned out to be well founded: The promoters of the underground garage project had not abandoned their plan for a garage on Rittenhouse Square after all.[13] On October 5 the Philadelphia Parking Authority issued bonds to finance a parking garage at 1845 Walnut Street—this one above ground, on the site of the former Sturgis/Ingersoll home.

To some observers it seemed that CCRA's effort had backfired—that the thwarting of an invisible garage beneath Rittenhouse Square had led instead to the construction of an unsightly aboveground garage facing the Square. But in fact there was an important distinction between the two garage projects. As the Square's devotees perceived from long experience, in the life of a city, buildings will come and go—some more appealing than others. But the Square itself was unique, and the integrity of its boundaries was a cause worth defending.

By the 1950s the old high-rise apartment buildings erected to such chagrin in the 1920s had become accepted parts of the landscape, even cherished as "prewar buildings," in real estate vernacular. Town houses and their inhabitants no longer established the social tone on the Square, with one notable exception. In 1950 a Victorian house along the Square's southwest corner, formerly owned by Lisa Norris Elkins but bequeathed to the Art Museum, was purchased by Henry McIlhenny, curator of decorative arts at the Philadelphia Museum of Art since 1935 and himself a collector of great repute. McIlhenny's new home promptly became what a fellow curator called "an extraordinarily hospitable extension of the Museum"[14]—a repository for some of the city's finest privately owned decorative art and paintings, as well as a gathering place for the eclectic assortment of art aficionados and celebrities who counted themselves among McIlhenny's circle of friends.

To the pop artist Andy Warhol (who apparently never heard of Stokowski), Henry McIlhenny was "the only person in Philadelphia with glamour."[15] Sundays at his home were described by the English poet Stephen Spender:

Sunday with Henry McIlhenny. It was delightful to be in his house for twenty-four hours, with a really comfortable bed, servants, excellent food and Henry's exhilarating conversation and gossip. I suppose the key to H.'s personality is that he counts his prodigious blessings every day, is enormously grateful for them, and lives up to them.[16]

Notwithstanding the exodus to the suburbs, one downtown developer now concluded that the Philadelphia market was ripe for sophisticated city living. In the late 1940s, Kevy K. Kaiserman and his contractor partner Matthew McCloskey proposed the construction of two modern apartment buildings, the Square's first since the Depression. These structures would offer central air conditioning and, at the Claridge, a basement garage and a $400,000 restaurant operated by Longchamps of New York. But perhaps their greatest selling point was their apartment views overlooking the Square. In the past, residents had peeked discreetly on the Square through narrow curtained windows, in keeping with the Old Philadelphia notion that gawking from one's windows was vulgar. Kaiserman, by contrast, proposed panoramic windows wide enough to create the impression of a glass wall in one's living room.

The new structures would, the developers promised, become Philadelphia's hallmark of sophisticated city living. But first they would have to run a gauntlet of zoning issues raised by a newly resurgent and apprehensive Center City Residents Association.

When Kaiserman unveiled his plan for the twenty-one-story Savoy on the south side of the Square in December 1949, he encountered a groundswell of sentimental resistance: This modernistic high-rise (one of the first in the country), with ribbonlike horizontal lines on its front facade, would displace the cozy row of houses that Henry James's prose had immortalized in 1904—including the homes of Jules Mastbaum, the actress Fanny Kemble, and Dr. J. William White. Even residents who knew little of James, Mastbaum, and White argued that the Savoy's design was inappropriate for the Square.

"I was shocked when I saw the architect's conception of the apartment," commented the developer John McShain, who had acquired the more traditional Barclay Hotel in 1940 and lived in its penthouse with his wife.[17] "Nothing like that predominates in the Square."[18] McShain was chairman of the Zoning Board of Adjustment as well as a rival of Kaiserman's contractor partner Matthew

McCloskey. On Rittenhouse Square, home to so many civic movers and shakers, conflicts of interest were common, and objective expressions of judgment were the exception.

A month after Kaiserman and McCloskey announced the Savoy, they unveiled plans for a second and much larger high-rise, the 25-story Claridge, on the east side of the Square, with 482 apartments. As he had done with the Savoy, Walter Hudson of CCRA asked Kaiserman to modify his plan for the Claridge so as to provide "something that more nearly conforms with the architecture of the Square" (Figure 8.2).[19]

Yet in fact the "architecture of the Square" was changing even as he spoke. The three beloved old town houses on the proposed Savoy property had not been

■ FIGURE 8.2 *The Rittenhouse Claridge, with its modern, controversial ribbon widows, was the Square's first post-war building.* (Photograph by Nancy Heinzen.)

used as dwellings in years: Since 1925 they had been occupied by the Eastern Baptist Theological Seminary, and after the seminary moved to suburban Wynnewood in 1942, they stood empty for seven years.[20] Something would replace them; the only question was what, and when. Kaiserman shrugged off objections to the Savoy as "the same resistance that confronts any new idea."[21]

When CCRA met to discuss the Savoy project in February 1950, some speakers supported it, arguing that Kaiserman's project would be better than the "rat-infested vacant lots" it would replace.[22] CCRA's attorney Paul Chalfin himself said the Savoy project "represents progress in residential living in the center of the city."[23] A *Bulletin* columnist the next day called it "a trifle odd that a few more skyscrapers were somehow supposed to ruin the antique charm of the place," especially since "the sedate old aspect of Rittenhouse Square has been gone for years."[24]

Kaiserman, defending the Savoy and the Claridge before the Zoning Board, argued that "the architecture surrounding the Square is a conglomeration" and contended the Savoy would "lend dignity to the square."[25] He assured CCRA that the building's ribbonlike horizontal lines would be broken up by vertical lines that were not visible in the architect's drawing.

But the design aspect of the high-rises was not the only concern they raised; many neighbors worried about increased population density around the Square as well. "Because of the tenants in the new apartments," the *Bulletin* columnist puckishly suggested, "they will have to put traffic officers along the paths to handle the perambulator jams that will occur. The benches will have to be replaced by grandstands, and a flock of goats will not suffice to accommodate the toddlers."[26] (In fact, few toddlers were to be found among the families moving into the new apartments.)

Another concern was the traditional concept of the Square as a healthful oasis with access to air and light—a peaceful respite from the hurly-burly of the streets. Both the Savoy and the Claridge exceeded the city zoning code's existing height and open-air restrictions. At the same CCRA meeting in February 1950, a speaker was applauded when she said the proposed Savoy building will "cut off sunshine and air from Rittenhouse Square."[27]

Yet ultimately CCRA acquiesced to both projects. Indeed, CCRA sponsored a ceremony to celebrate the joint opening of the Claridge and Savoy in August 1951. A crowd of several thousand gathered in the sun-drenched Square to hear David Walker, Pennsylvania's secretary of labor and industry, describe the two buildings as symbols of Philadelphia's recent progress.[28]

The opening of the Savoy and the Claridge cleared the way for a third new luxury high-rise on the Square's west side. In the mid-1950s the developer Ephraim Frankel acquired and razed the J. B. Lippincott mansion, built in 1866 on the corner of Locust Street, to make way for what became 220 West Rittenhouse Square. Frankel enticed the Lippincott mansion's ground-floor tenant, the Philadelphia City Institute (since 1944 a branch of the Free Library system), to occupy the ground floor of his new high-rise, in effect ensuring the continued presence of yet another major cultural institution along the Square's border. Frankel also renovated the Wellington on Walnut Street from naval supply offices back into apartments.

The eagerness of developers to build still more high-rises revived community concerns about the loss of light and air. Shortly after the Savoy and Claridge opened, another apartment building, then tentatively called the Rittenhouse Terrace, was proposed on the Square's west side by the New York development firm Webb and Knapp. The question of whether this building should be "set back" from the Square to compensate for its thirty-two-story height was one of several zoning controversies related to the Rittenhouse Terrace that persisted for years. Not until March 1955, after a "stormy discussion," did CCRA approve the project —but by a narrow vote of 63 to 56, and without resolving the setback issue.[29]

Yet the legal costs of gaining the various approvals had drained much of the developer's financing, and consequently the Rittenhouse Terrace project stagnated.

In June 1955, from his penthouse on South Rittenhouse Square, Michael Francis Doyle wrote to Paul M. Chalfin, president of CCRA, about the Terrace site:

> Your particular attention is called to the condition of two properties on the west side of Rittenhouse Square below Locust Street. Both of these buildings have their fronts torn out for many months and are an eyesore and disgrace to Philadelphia. Nothing is being done about it either by the owners or by your Association.

Chalfin replied reassuringly that the properties were under agreement of sale and that a large apartment house was planned for the site.[30] But as of April 1959, CCRA and neighboring residents were still arguing parking and setback issues with the Terrace developers before the city's Zoning Board of Adjustment. The builders proposed a higher structure with less parking than zoning laws permitted. Existing law required a stair-step design that would allow neighboring properties to have access to light and air. Clark Hanna, attorney for the residents, claimed that the proposed building would reduce light by one-third. The developer admitted that light would be lost but said the building would reflect sunlight on some properties "which have never seen sunlight."

Ultimately the residents won the setback issue but lost the battle on parking: The Zoning Board approved an amended application. But still the fight continued.[31] The Terrace's next-door high-rise, the Crillon, objected that the Terrace would wrap itself around the Crillon. It was February 1960 before the Crillon agreed to a settlement with the Terrace developers.[32]

In 1961—six years after Doyle had complained about the "eyesore and disgrace"—the Terrace project appeared to be bogged down yet again when Webb and Knapp withdrew from the project.[33] But construction finally got under way under a new partnership led by Matthew McCloskey, who gave the beleaguered building a new name: the Dorchester (Figure 8.3).

■ FIGURE 8.3 *The Dorchester Apartments, opened in 1961, initiated the second wave of modern apartments.* (Photograph by Nancy Heinzen.)

Ultimately, great plans and grand buildings matter less to a community's viability than its human fabric. While real estate developers aimed for the sky, organizations like the Center City Residents Association were left to cope with the small, petty, frustrating, and often intractable nuisances that persisted at street level.

For example, as early as 1748, Peter Kalm had found the number of wild pigeons in Philadelphia "beyond conception," and hunters had been sent to Governor's Woods to shoot the birds. Two hundred years later, the descendants of those pigeons—the original residents of Rittenhouse Square—still persisted in claiming their ancestral birthright. No longer were these birds desirable as a food source; now they were feared as potential carriers of disease. From time to time the city had fought them with whatever resources it could muster, without success.

"The town has tried to chase them with red paint, with wild hawks, with sandblasting, with water hoses, with gas, with nets, with wire screens, with sodium silicate, with mercury lighting, with electronic hotfoots, with toy lizards," wrote the Philadelphia journalist Frank Brookhouser in 1957.[34]

World War II had barely ended in 1945 when the city launched its own war on pigeons with passage of a law against feeding pigeons on the Square. But the law was not enforced, and when the newly formed Center City Residents Association complained about lax enforcement three years later, Fairmount Park commissioner Raymond Rosen explained why: The Square's guards, he said, "know all the residents of the Square intimately, and it is hard for them to enforce every regulation to the letter. . . . It's like one big family there."[35]

After polling its members in 1951, CCRA found that an overwhelming majority favored eliminating the pigeons from the Square.[36] Precisely how to go about it was another question. Some residents favored killing the birds humanely, others wanted to starve them, and at least one suggested destroying the pigeons' eggs, so that in due time the birds would die off; she volunteered to locate nests for the authorities.[37]

In a joint report, CCRA and the Rittenhouse Square Improvement Association blamed the lax efforts on both the new apartment houses around the Square and visitors to the Square from outlying neighborhoods.[38] Whatever the explanation, the pigeon problem proved intractable.

However much energy and newsprint the pigeon issue consumed, it was dwarfed by the issue of dogs in the Square. Throughout the 1950s and 1960s, both the Fairmount Park Commission and CCRA convened special committees on dogs (although, to be sure, no one advocated their extinction).[39] A 1956 ordinance forbade dogs "to commit any nuisance either in Rittenhouse Square or on the sidewalks thereof" and required that dogs brought into the Square be leashed and confined to the walks. "Curb your dog" signs were installed by CCRA,[40] but owners ignored the signs, and dog deposits continued to be found everywhere.

Frederic Mann, Philadelphia's city representative and commerce director as well as a property owner on the Square's south side and a resident of the Barclay, jumped into the dog debate in 1957 when he suggested a "comfort station" for dogs, discreetly fenced and hidden by shrubs.[41] That proposal failed to pass.

In the spring of 1963, Fairmount Park Director W. H. Noble banned dogs from the Square altogether, on the ground that they dug holes that destroyed lawns and trees. That remedy galvanized the Square's dog lovers. "For twenty-three years it has been one of my great pleasures to walk with my dogs in Rittenhouse Square," one member wrote to CCRA. "Today five guards were there to enforce this new ruling. Let us know exactly who is responsible for this deplorable situation so that the hundreds of dog lovers may voice their protests in the coming elections."[42] Another resident claimed that dogs were being unfairly singled out: "Would you like to see how the Park looks after The Flower show? People actually put stakes and bore holes in the lawn to put up their stands. Where are we living? City of Brotherly Love or Russia or Germany? . . . By the way is there anything we can do to exterminate the squirrels? They dig too."[43] Leonard Wolf, president of the CCRA, wrote to Mayor James Tate, contending that dogs on leashes could not legally be banned from the Square.[44]

The dogs, like the pigeons, soon returned to the Square, and the debate continued unresolved for more than a generation to follow.

EVEN AFTER THE SAVOY replaced three abandoned town houses on the Square's south side in 1951, a vacant lot remained between the Savoy and 1830 South Rittenhouse. In 1960, Walter Hudson pointed out to CCRA's Rittenhouse Square committee that this "eyesore" belonged to Frederic Mann. Such a prominent property owner, Hudson noted, could "be difficult and he can be very cooperative. If approached through the idea of civic betterment, since he is a city official, he might consent to some sort of planting or beautification of the area."[45]

But Mann had his own ideas. In 1961 he announced plans to build a luxury co-op on the site, to be developed by his son-in-law. But these plans never reached fruition. Instead Mann took the path followed by other Center City property owners stuck with tax bills on unproductive property: In 1964 he won permission to convert the site to a parking lot.[46] This approval by the City Planning Commission, of which Mann was himself a member, outraged residents, who feared the lot would become a permanent fixture. Even if it was "attractively built," as Mann promised, they wanted no part of it. Mann, a father bountiful to dozens of musicians and singers, appears to have been tone deaf to the wrath that parking lots engendered in the community.

The publicity was an embarrassment to Mann, who threatened to quit city government.[47] But the lot would remain until the 1970s, when Raymond Perelman would build a sleek, ultramodern apartment building there: 1820 South Rittenhouse Square, with huge apartments, many of which took up entire floors.

Slowly the balance on the Square was tipping from commercial usage back to residential. Such was the escalating value of real estate on the Square that in

September 1968 a bid was made to buy the Church of the Holy Trinity itself—and while the church ultimately rejected the offer, four years later it did sell the adjoining Cassatt and Lippincott mansions on West Rittenhouse Square.[48] The Academy of Notre Dame, also on the west side of the Square for nearly a century, finally got an offer it couldn't refuse: In 1967 this last private school in the Rittenhouse Square neighborhood sold its property for $1 million and followed the other private schools out of the city to the Main Line, where its high school had already functioned since 1943.

The luxury apartment building planned for its site (as well as the site of the Cassatt and Lippincott mansions) was the first apartment complex to be proposed in four years, but because of a lack of adequate financing, it would not be completed for more than two decades. The 1960s building boom in "ritzy Rittenhouse Square" ended as abruptly as it had begun.

THROUGHOUT THE POSTWAR PERIOD and into the 1950s, the Barclay continued to flourish as the social center of the Square and, by extension, of Philadelphia's high society. It was home to the Philadelphia Orchestra's music director, Eugene Ormandy, as well as the prominent builder John McShain. Before the afternoon concert on Fridays, the Barclay dining room was "always monopolized by smartly dressed lady subscribers or members of committees, in from the country."[49] In the evenings, guests in fur coats and tuxedos pulled up in their big chrome-bumpered cars.[50]

Even during the 1960s and 1970s. the Barclay's cocktail lounge remained the most sophisticated spot in town. Couples chatted quietly in low-lit corners while Cole Porter tunes drifted from the piano across the room. Charity balls, coming-out parties, and wedding receptions continued to be held in the ballroom and in the mirrored Mirage Room on the second floor, overlooking the Square. The glitter tended to camouflage the fact that the Barclay's affluent clientele, like the hotel itself, was ever so slowly aging and dying off.

WHILE CCRA WRESTLED with real estate development, pigeons, and dogs through the 1950s, the Rittenhouse Square Improvement Association remained active as a private planning and fund-raising organization. But in 1960, after forty-seven years as an independent organization, the Rittenhouse Square Improvement Association became the Women's Committee of the Fairmount Park Art Association. At the same time, the Fairmount Park Commission maintained legal jurisdiction over the Square as well as financial responsibility for its upkeep. An underlying tension persisted between the advocacy groups and the Park Commission, whose allocation of limited funds within the citywide park system was always a contentious issue.

By this time the number of annual events held on the Square—and the consequent wear and tear—had increased manyfold since the first Flower Market was held in 1914. The annual Clothesline Art Show continued. The annual Christmas tree lighting, started by the Penn Athletic Club (Figure 8.4), subsequently became a CCRA winter activity that involved carolers, university glee clubs, and, in 1967, even an appearance by the contralto Marian Anderson.[51] The traditional Easter Parade became institutionalized under CCRA with a pageant, high school choirs, and a display of lilies on a cross in the center of the Square (apparently without objection from the Square's sizable Jewish population). Eventually the Walnut Street Businessmen's Association took it over, bringing what a magazine called "a more festival atmosphere, with prizes for original fancy costumes and leading styles in fashions."[52]

In addition to annual events, many one-time events were held. In 1953 the Red Cross got permission to place two large Marine Corps tents on the Square for its blood drives. Several thousand persons jammed Rittenhouse Square in a single

■ FIGURE 8.4 *The Penn Athletic Club sponsored the Square's first Christmas tree in 1930. Note the windows of the dining room that looked out over the Square.*
(The Library Company of Philadelphia.)

afternoon to donate blood for the armed services and civilians in Korea as well as for the fight against a polio outbreak.[53]

The good news for Rittenhouse Square in these events was the Square's popularity among Philadelphians of many walks of life. The bad news, as Park Commissioner Raymond Rosen put it as early as 1951, was the "terrific beating" the Square and especially its lawns took from all these public events.[54]

Walter Hudson, speaking for CCRA in 1953, complained that the Square was being neglected by the Fairmount Park Commission. Rosen, in turn, blamed the problem on drought—something more likely to be noticed by horticulturists than by high-rise dwellers. Each year, when grass was planted, he explained, pigeons feasted on the seeds and dogs trampled new grass before it could fully take root. Year after year, the same problems, the same complaints, and the same responses occurred in a predictable pattern among CCRA, the Fairmount Park Commission, and the Rittenhouse Square Improvement Association.

Nevertheless, in 1961 a landmark book called *The Death and Life of Great American Cities*, by the high priestess of urban planning, Jane Jacobs, celebrated Rittenhouse Square as one of North America's best urban spaces—"a beloved, successful, much-used space, one of Philadelphia's greatest assets."[55]

At some point between 1944 and 1951, the Square's reflecting pool ceased to be filled with water. Its stagnant water, Fairmount Park Commissioner Raymond Rosen said, made it a "breeding place for mosquitoes."[56] In 1952 the pool was refilled, but the water still tended to become stagnant.[57] The Improvement Association was still wrestling with the problem the following year when nature abruptly revised the group's agenda.

Philadelphia was suffering from drought and heat when, on July 19, 1953, eighty-mile-per-hour winds roared through the city. On Rittenhouse Square, fallen leaves and branches were ankle deep. Eight mature trees were toppled. A large maple was left leaning precariously over the walk by the entrance at Eighteenth and Locust streets. All these trees had to be replaced, but planting was delayed because of the drought and the difficulty of finding replacement trees large enough to balance with old ones. Yet the biggest storm was still to come.

The next year brought Hazel, a hurricane that altered the landscape throughout southeastern Pennsylvania and much of the East Coast. More than a thousand trees came down in Philadelphia.[58] But the indomitable Marion Rivinus perceived in Hazel a "blessing in disguise" for Rittenhouse Square: Because the trees had not been replaced from the earlier storm of 1953, and Hazel had brought down so many trees in the Square's center allée, the allée could now be planted with chestnut trees all of identical size.[59]

IN 1950 A RITTENHOUSE SQUARE resident named William Reinhardt wrote a letter to CCRA that listed "things we should fight for."[60] It was an astute concept: Some civic issues (like the proposed underground garage) have always galvanized public interest and support more effectively than others. Reinhardt was concerned about safety in the Square and its surroundings. But throughout the Square's history, nothing has raised the hackles of CCRA and the Rittenhouse Square Improvement Association more than any sort of encroachment onto the Square as it was originally conceived by William Penn and planned by Thomas Holme.

In April 1954—just three years after the underground garage was defeated—the Philadelphia Transit Company revived a twenty-year-old proposal to lay trolley tracks across the Square's northwest corner, opposite Holy Trinity, to "shake the kinks out" of the Route 17 trolley line down Nineteenth Street. A transit company spokesman said that this corner cut was "imperative" as the solution to traffic problems on Walnut Street. The trolley lane would go from the spot where Nineteenth Street dead-ends into Walnut Street, cross the Square diagonally, and then intersect with West Rittenhouse Square midway between Walnut and Locust streets.[61] In practical terms, nearly one-third of the Square would be lost (Figure 8.5).

Similar intrusions had already reconfigured William Penn's other original squares in order to accommodate traffic, something Penn could not have imagined in his wildest dreams. A similar cut in 1947 had chopped off the northwest corner of Washington Square. Logan Square was decimated in the 1920s and turned into a traffic circle to enhance the new Ben Franklin Parkway leading to the equally new Art Museum. Parts of Franklin Square were reconfigured to accommodate traffic to and from the Ben Franklin Bridge. The trolley cut through Rittenhouse Square, first proposed in 1933, had been abandoned only because of its cost in the midst of the Depression, and initially there seemed no reason in 1954 to doubt that the voracious needs of modern transportation would have their way with Rittenhouse Square just as they had with the others.

The corner cut was approved by the city's managing director but required approval by the Fairmount Park Commission as well.[62] Here CCRA chose to make its stand.

The organization issued an urgent appeal to members to fight this intrusion into the Square's original boundaries. Its members, sounding much like the Founding Fathers in 1776, responded by passing a resolution that pledged "the

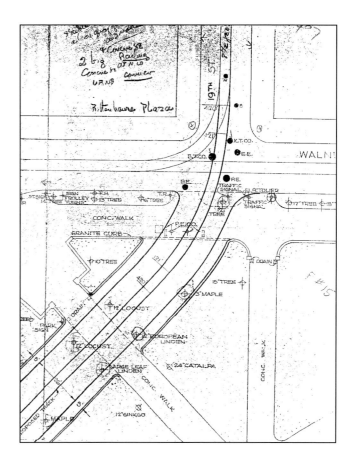

■ FIGURE 8.5 *The city's 1954 plan for cutting off the northwestern corner of Rittenhouse Square to ease the traffic flow.* (Temple University Libraries, Urban Archives, Philadelphia, Pennsylvania.)

use of all means at its command to preserve Rittenhouse Square inviolate and to withstand any and all attempts of misguided persons or groups to defile it."[63] Confronted with this aroused revolt by some of its most articulate and influential citizens, the city took the path of least resistance and abandoned the project to invest its slender capital resources elsewhere.

That the city's resources were limited, of course, was an important factor in keeping the Square's boundaries intact. In a conversation with the author, Bruce Lavery, curator of architecture at the Philadelphia Athenaeum, commented that economic recession is a great friend of preservation.

※

BUT SOME THINGS remained beyond a mere neighborhood's control. In the 1960s Rittenhouse Square became a microcosm of a society in the throes of changing global mores. A new postwar generation reached adolescence and young adulthood with no memory of either the Depression or World War II. Where young people in the late 1940s and 1950s had venerated their elders for bequeathing them a world of peace and prosperity, this new generation of "baby boomers" took peace and prosperity for granted; instead they rebelled against a world they perceived as conformist, materialistic, and racist.

Resistance to racial segregation and the Vietnam war became their rallying points. In communes, coffeehouses, and public parks, long-haired "beatniks" (later "hippies") strove to create a counterculture that rejected money and social convention in favor of free love, drugs, and rock music; their mottos—so threatening to their elders—were "Make love, not war" and "Turn on, tune in, drop out."

Rittenhouse Square, as Philadelphia's most popular public gathering place, became a major focal point in this culture war. "The park scene is fun," one hippie told a journalist. "It's a happening." Rittenhouse Square was their preferred gathering place, many hippies said, because it was convenient and also residential. "You're in the center of people who are way above. They are the golden people who cry about our being here. We accept everybody and don't like people to look down on us." Other groups, eager to make public statements of one sort or another, appeared on the weekends as well: black-power advocates, poets, artists, intellectuals, dropouts, kids with family problems, and just plain social misfits.[64]

Soon outraged citizens were writing letters to newspapers and to CCRA decrying drug use and other "indecent, immoral" behavior in the Square. One complained of "people lying on the grass in various stages of undress, ruining the lawn, littering the Square until it looks like a garbage dump."[65] Another reported to CCRA that "Saturday night it was absolutely revolting to either pass through or sit in the square. Furthermore DOZENS of half clad youths were spread full-length all over the grass" (Figure 8.6).[66]

Contrary to the stereotype, many young people who frequented the Square defied easy categorization. To them, Rittenhouse Square and other friendly venues nearby—most notably the Gilded Cage, a coffeehouse and folk music nightspot at Twenty-first and Rittenhouse Square streets—were places where they had found a community of acceptance among one another.[67] At other gathering places, like the Second Fret, at Nineteenth and Sansom streets, or the Proscenium on Walnut Street, listeners could hear unknown performers, some of whom—like Joni Mitchell, Judy Collins, and Arlo Guthrie—subsequently became symbols of this generation.

The author Tom Purdom, who would not characterize himself as a hippie, later recalled the Gilded Cage as "a perfect institution for a young writer who worked at a full-time job and wrote for two hours every night. Once you became a regular, you could drop in at any time and find a few people you knew." To many people, Purdom noted, "coffeehouses were inhabited by 'Bohemians,' 'beatniks,' and other strange types," but "most of the people I met at the Gilded Cage were fully employed young people who lived in the neighborhood around Philadelphia's most popular downtown gathering place, Rittenhouse Square."[68]

■ FIGURE 8.6 *The cartoonist Alfred Bendiner takes a light view of the counterculture, which in the 1960s was a polarizing topic among residents.*
(The Architectural Archives, University of Pennsylvania.)

But the Square was also, of course, home to some of the city's most powerful movers and shakers. Frederic Mann, who lived in the Barclay, described the Square to the press as a "jungle where people could not venture at night." By 1963, Mann, then chairman of the Fairmount Park Commission's Rittenhouse Square Committee, called for a crackdown on "undesirables." Harold Schick, Fairmount Park director, said he was inundated with calls to "do something" about the kids (Figure 8.7).[69]

As Philadelphians had discovered during the Depression in the 1930s, defining "undesirables" was a tricky proposition, as the American Civil Liberties Union

■ Figure 8.7
College students
burning draft cards
during a 1970s
anti-war rally in
the Square.
(Temple University
Libraries,
Urban Archives,
Philadelphia,
Pennsylvania.)

was quick to point out. The older generation's demands also conflicted with a growing national trend to liberalize access to parks and other public places. One result was the removal of the Square's "keep off the grass" signs, which effectively made it legal for young people to lie together on the Square without breaking the law.

When a force of sixty-five policemen rounded up thirty-four suspected "beat-nik type" marijuana users in the Square in 1966, District Attorney Arlen Specter announced that "a real narcotics problem in Rittenhouse Square" had been "broken up by this raid." (Ultimately, only three of those arrested were charged with dealing in marijuana.)[70]

A more nuanced assessment was provided by Albert Levitt, supervisor of narcotics addicts for the State Parole Board. Rittenhouse Square itself, he said, was not so much a haven for addicts as a refuge for those who will "mature out of this stage." "The young rebels and those who shout the loudest against them need each other," Levitt added. "That's why these situations develop in places like Rittenhouse Square and not in an empty lot in Eastwick." That is, people eager to express themselves gravitated toward Rittenhouse Square because it was the city's equivalent of Hyde Park corner in London. Only the passage of time, Levitt predicted, would "do something about Rittenhouse Square."[71]

Of course the "hippie invasion" of the 1960s addressed a larger urban issue in free societies: how to maintain public standards of behavior without infringing on personal liberties. Like a drop of ink in an otherwise pure glass of water, the hippie presence might have destroyed the Square's fragile social fabric; yet the curious thing about this episode is that nothing of the sort happened. Many of these same young people, following graduation, would move to the Square's neighborhood, buy business suits and perhaps a briefcase, and become conventional citizens.

"Personally I couldn't care less whether the hippies use Rittenhouse Square for a social gathering place or not," a resident named Frank Tooke wrote to CCRA. "The Square is big enough to provide me with a relatively comfortable bench in some quiet corner so that I am not forced to look at shaggy haircuts and dirty jeans."[72]

Tooke noted that William Penn had prescribed the four Philadelphia squares as public places, with all the risks that designation implies. Tooke pondered "what that great freedom lover Billy Penn would say if he could come back and spend an evening in the Square! Will you hazard a guess with me that he would probably be rather pleased?"

This guess would have been mistaken. William Penn conceived of his city not as a center of self-expression or pleasure but as a place to conduct business and commerce. His squares were intended for the relief of people who, for whatever reason, had to endure the worldly atmosphere of cities. Penn and his family, given the choice, had resided at Pennsbury, in Bucks County, many miles from Philadelphia, in the belief that country life was more wholesome. After nearly three hundred years, Penn's vision had become a tabula rasa for anyone inclined to make use of it.

The Millennium

[1968–2009]

By the mid-1970s the Vietnam war was over and many members of the protest generation, having aged a few years in the meantime, turned their countercultural energies in other creative directions, such as art studio co-ops and a blossoming of innovative restaurants. Some former hippies were now providing *nouvelle cuisine* to those who had feared them just a few years earlier. What was once "undesirable" became "normal."

The overcrowding on Rittenhouse Square that was feared as a result of the new apartments built in the 1950s never came to pass. On the surface, Philadelphia seemed a place where people were moving out, not in. The city's population peaked just above the two million mark in 1950 and dropped steadily thereafter. Industries that had enriched Philadelphia as well as many Rittenhouse Square residents continued to close or move. In 1970 the once-omnipotent Pennsylvania Railroad went bankrupt.[1] Throughout the 1970s, as the proposed Rittenhouse Hotel and Condominium on the Square's west side struggled to avoid bankruptcy, the Square's devotees endured the awkward sight of concrete-faced iron columns jutting like huge stalagmites from cavernous concrete subfloors on a construction site once occupied by the Cassatt mansion and Notre Dame Academy.

Rittenhouse Square's bygone elite, mourned the *New York Times* in a 1974 "eulogy," had been replaced by "black schoolchildren, young idlers, old wastrels and homosexuals of all ages."[2]

Yet a discerning reporter who delved beneath the surface might have found evidence of a new awakening. The highly regarded Albert M. Greenfield School, Center City's first public elementary school in generations, opened in 1959. Those black schoolchildren noticed by the *Times* reporter in 1974 were, for the most part, Greenfield students whose highly motivated parents cared enough about education to bus their children to Greenfield from distant sections of the city. Those apparent young idlers were in fact on the cusp of launching a restaurant renaissance and a boom in local art galleries. And, as the *Times* itself acknowledged many years later, homosexuals in Philadelphia and other urban downtowns had come to constitute an important bulwark of upper-middle-class stability in a time of white flight to the suburbs; indeed, gay men and women were among Rittenhouse Square's most active and generous supporters.

Thanks in no small part to these supposed outcast groups, Rittenhouse Square and its surroundings remained an island of relative stability in Philadelphia, with a population that actually increased slightly through the 1970s.[3]

As Philadelphia prepared for the U.S. Bicentennial Celebration in 1976, Rittenhouse Square found itself out of money and without an adequate fund-raising arm. The Rittenhouse Square Improvement Association, the Square's major source of fund-raising since 1913, had become the Women's Committee of the Fairmount Park Art Association in 1960, taking its funds and duties with it.[4]

To spruce up the Square for the Bicentennial, a new group called Friends of Rittenhouse Square was founded in 1976 by a small cadre headed by the developers Ken Kaiserman (Kevy's son) and Jack Wolgin. Both men had vested interests in the Square as property owners, and Kaiserman lived and worked at the Savoy, which his father had built in 1951.[5] Wolgin had purchased the Cassatt and Notre Dame land on the Square's west side to build a high-rise hotel/condo, then in limbo. At first the two men and a few neighbors provided most of the organization's funds, but the Friends soon grew to a membership of six hundred.[6]

Between 1976 and 1982, the Friends planted azaleas around the Square's perimeter, developed and helped pay for new lighting, and (in tandem with CCRA) got the Square included in the National Register of Historic Places—a listing which, in theory at least, would protect the Square from radical physical changes.

Perhaps most important, the Friends lobbied the city to erect a fence that enclosed the Square for the first time in nearly a century. The psychological effect was immense, separating the Square from the bustling city around it and once again creating a feeling of safety and tranquility.

Although the Square remained the technical responsibility of the Fairmount Park Commission, in 1982 the Friends hired a full-time gardener, with Fairmount Park providing seeds, plants, tools, and fertilizer. Under the supervision of George Patton, a Center City landscape architect, overgrowth was cleared and, for the first time in several years, the reflecting pool was filled. The sprinkler system installed in the 1950s was upgraded, and a new plan for paving the central terrace was presented.[7] Between the combination of the Friends' prodding and financial support, in the ensuing years the Park Commission replaced benches, patched up the reflecting pool and fountain, and installed a new irrigation system and new walkways.[8]

As in the past, the Friends worked in conjunction with the Fairmount Park Commission; but now it was clear that the Friends would have to raise the lion's share of the funds to carry out any plans. "We couldn't run the parks today without the support of the Friends groups," Fairmount Park's director of operations, Jim Donaghy, acknowledged in 1991.[9]

This involvement of private citizens, of course, was a continuing tradition on the Square: It extended back not just to the formation of the Rittenhouse Square Improvement Association in 1913 but all the way back to 1816, when private citizens lent the city $800 for a fence around the Square.

After two fund-raising events hosted by Henry McIlhenny at his fabled residence, the Friends of Rittenhouse Square announced their presence as a formidable civic force on the evening of June 23, 1984, with their first major fund-raising event: the Ball on the Square. The ball was promoted as a celebration of the three hundredth anniversary of Thomas Holme's grid plan, which first visualized William Penn's five historic squares. The ball's chairman, Arnold H. Rosenberg, who lived at the Dorchester, repeated the wish of Mrs. G. Gordon Meade Large at the first Flower Market in 1914: "We want this to be the beginning of a tradition."[10] The Flower Market, of course, had raised funds for the Square too; but it also raised money for children's charities. The Ball on the Square, Rosenberg noted, was held solely "to raise the kind of money it takes to preserve this incredible urban amenity." Tickets to the first ball ranged from $150 to $1,000 per couple. More than three hundred were sold, and the ball reached its announced goal of raising $50,000.

Much like the Flower Market at its inception, the ball was a society event. Newspaper photographers snapped photos of Esther Klein and Gloria Etting, the honorary chairwomen, as they arrived at "Eve of Midsummer Night." Artificial fog swirled around the arrivals as characters from *A Midsummer Night's Dream* welcomed the guests. "Women wore dark cocktail dresses," the *New York Times* reported, and "some brightly colored floor-length dresses in cool fabrics. Many of the men wore black tie, with perhaps half in white dinner jackets."[11] It was, said Gloria Etting, "a moment of great resurgence."[12]

The following year the ball added a mammoth yellow tent lined with white tufted netting, a gift of Edward Lipkin, who lived in one of the last town houses—the nineteenth-century home of Dr. Lankenau at 1804 on the Square's south side. In subsequent years, the ball became a permanent fixture as well as one of the social highlights of each summer.[13] By 1998, tickets cost at least $600 per couple, and the Friends were contributing a major portion of the Square's yearly upkeep.

Over the years the ball's fund-raising has paid for weekly landscaping service (at a cost of more than $70,000 per year), seasonal cleanup and planting, an additional Fairmount Park employee on weekends in warm weather, doggie bags, and spring flower plantings. In a cooperative venture with the Friends, in 1991 the city installed new street lights bordering the Square. Funds donated by the Friends also paid the city for extra trash collection on a daily basis during the summer.[14] Benches in the Square were replaced with teak—that is, splinter-free—benches from England, each bench adorned with a plaque dedicated to a donor who paid for this tiny bit of immortality. Through other donations, the Friends installed a guardhouse in the center of the Square, an exact copy of the kiosks that had stood in Fairmount Park during the 1876 Centennial celebration. In 1999 Paul Cret's tile mural, missing since 1914, was replicated from his original drawings.

THE BIRTH OF the Friends of Rittenhouse Square in the 1970s took place in tandem with the dawn of a new real estate phenomenon. Landlords of the grand old prewar high-rises and the sleek modern postwar high-rises alike, unable to raise rents sufficiently to compensate for skyrocketing inflation and energy costs, began converting their apartment buildings to condominiums, in effect selling individual apartments (usually) to their tenants. This process forced tenants who had paid reasonable rents for years or decades to scrape up large down payments in order to remain in their homes. But they now enjoyed an equity stake in properties whose value was likely to appreciate faster than many of their other investments.

For the neighborhood as a whole, an unexpected by-product of these conversions was a psychological change: Residents who had previously thought of themselves as tenants now became owners with a vested interest in maintaining their property values and the neighborhood's integrity.

Fifteen years after its foundation was dug, the five-star Rittenhouse Hotel and Condominium finally opened its doors on the Square's west side in 1989—although by then it had passed to its third developer, a consortium headed by David Marshall. With this final anchor in place and the Friends a viable organization, Rittenhouse Square's long and difficult resurrection seemed ensured.

"It's working now," Gary Levinson, president of the Friends and a resident of the Dorchester, declared in 1989. His guideline, he said, was the mix of people who used the Square in the course of a day: early exercisers, then workers, older folks, then mothers and toddlers, lunch, kids out of school, and evening after-dinner constitutionals.[15]

But in fact many of the same old nagging human and animal problems persisted, as they will inevitably wherever large numbers of fallible humans live and work together at close quarters. The initial sale of condos moved slowly, hampered by rising perceptions of crime, litter, and homeless people living on the streets. By the following year supporters of Friends of Rittenhouse Square were joining with business, community, and city officials in a task force to take back what they described as Center City "under siege."[16] In 1990 the Center City District was created as a self-taxing district to assist the financially strapped city government in keeping the downtown area (including the Rittenhouse Square neighborhood) clean, safe, and attractive.

AT THE DAWN of the 1990s the architectural border of the Square seemed threatened. Four different properties, each redolent with historical significance, were for sale on the Square as of January 1991:[17]

1. Henry McIlhenny's house on the southwest corner, one of the Square's last nineteenth-century homes, had long been famous for its architectural beauty, its world-class art collection, and its owner's social cachet. But after McIlhenny's death in 1986 the house sat vacant.[18]

2. Also for sale was the Rittenhouse Club building on Walnut Street, which included the outer walls of the original James Harper house. By 1991 the Rittenhouse Club's diminished membership could no longer use their large building, so the club rented space to various university clubs while flirting with the notion of moving to the smaller McIlhenny house across the Square. But the landmark status of the Rittenhouse Club building discouraged prospective buyers who might have renovated it for modern use.

3. By 1991 the Barclay, a bellwether for the area since 1929, had been on the market for two years; it would go through two bankruptcies before the end of the century.

4. The Van Rensselaer Mansion at Eighteenth and Walnut streets, which had already been reincarnated several times since it was vacated by the Penn Athletic Club in the mid-1950s, was again for sale, as was its next-door neighbor, the Alison Building.

The struggles of these four significant buildings were compounded by other ominous real estate situations on the Square. The Art Alliance, in the old Samuel Wetherill mansion on Eighteenth Street, had suspended operations. Negotiations for a sale of the Wellington had just fallen through. Condos around the Square were not moving.

"We've weathered this kind of thing before, and I think we will again," Center City Residents Association president Leonore Milhollen gamely told the *Inquirer*.[19] And she was right: Eighteen months later the pendulum swung, and the *Inquirer* reported a "revival" around Rittenhouse Square as condo buyers sought "a certain urban ambience."[20] This upswing was compounded in 1992 when Rittenhouse Square was designated a historic landmark by the city's Historical Commission; in 1995 the entire surrounding neighborhood was given "historic district status." These designations meant that neither the Square nor the exteriors of preexisting buildings could be altered without the commission's approval. Although the commission has at times breached this standard, this guarantee vastly enhanced the neighborhood's stability even as it brought yet another public entity—the Historical Commission—into the jumble of organizations with a stake in the Square.

By the late 1990s several organizations with different agendas sought to protect some aspect of the Square. These included Friends of Rittenhouse Square, CCRA, Center City District, Rittenhouse Row (a business-related group focused on Walnut Street), and the Historical Commission. It was about this time that Center City real estate brokers, always eager to exploit a hopeful trend, began using the term "Rittenhouse Square" in reference not only to the Square itself but also to the entire neighborhood from Broad Street west to the Schuylkill River.

THE BARCLAY'S REVIVAL took a while longer than its neighboring highrises. The young developer Jerry Pantelidis bought it in 1996 for conversion to condominiums but ran out of capital before finishing the job. In 1998, twenty-seven residents sued him over the building's failure to provide basic services, including access to hot water. Fred Mann's widow, Silvia, moved out after forty years.[21]

In June 1999 control of the Barclay passed into the hands of Allan Domb, who had made a niche for himself in a field that had not existed a generation earlier: as a broker who specialized in the sale of condominiums. Domb lacked development credentials but perceived what he called "a new optimism and new opportunities now" in the city. The Barclay appealed to Domb as an important piece of a bigger market: He saw affluent empty nesters moving from the suburbs into what he called the "vertical suburbs" around the Square: a neighborhood that offered health spas, shops, restaurants, convenience stores, rooftop swimming pools, culture, and a sense of community, all within walking distance. This was, of course, much the same vision that Walter Hudson of CCRA had championed half a century earlier. The area's number one attraction, Domb added, was Rittenhouse Square itself, "the jewel of the neighborhood."[22]

Domb's confident salesmanship attracted a who's who of new and old residents to the Barclay as condo buyers, offering them raw space in which to indulge their wildest design fantasies. Then he imposed a series of multimillion-dollar assessments for the necessary repairs to the building's infrastructure and told the Barclay's impatient residents they would have to endure a year or two more of chaos. "That's part of the building being reborn," he explained.[23] Within three years virtually every floor had been transformed into two or three stunning apartments, each one "more lavish than the next," *Philadelphia* magazine gushed in 2002.[24] Once again, the Barclay was a prestige address.

MIDNIGHT AT THE END of the tenth century A.D. had brought predictions of the end of the world throughout Christian Europe. Midnight at the end of the twentieth century brought fears of a global technological meltdown with the arrival of "Y2K"—shorthand for the year 2000. But in Philadelphia it brought Philadelphians of all stripes to their most logical gathering place for a "Luminaire in the Square" celebration on the last night of 1999. The event was promoted as a nineteenth-century-style fireworks display in recognition of the Square's founders (despite the lack of evidence that such a thing had ever taken place in the Square before).

Designated viewing areas in the Square were tightly packed by 7:00 P.M. People of all ages, bundled in scarves and parkas, stomped their feet and clapped gloved hands to keep warm, while casting about for better vantage points. As was customary at all Square events, the crowd was diverse, and close proximity instigated conversation among strangers. "What is a luminaire, anyway?" many asked each other.

Suddenly, a blast of a recorded Scott Joplin rag halted all conversation. Fountains of light gushed around the center oval. Sparkling jets of light rose and fell in unsynchronized accompaniment to the ragtime recording. Brilliant pinwheels revolved like spinning kaleidoscopes, showering sparks. There were no loud booms to make children cry and the elderly hold their ears. Old and young stood openmouthed at the rhythmic spewing fountains and whirling lollipops of light.

If the 7:00 P.M. performance seemed a prelude to the new millennium, the 2:00 A.M. show later that same night seemed a celebration in full swing. By now the children were home tucked in bed; this party was for the grownups. The earlier wool scarves gave way to fur coats and tuxedos. Champagne appeared, and glasses were passed among strangers.

Far above the Square, partygoers gathered behind frosty high-rise windows to look down on the scene. From fifteen or twenty stories up, it was like looking down into a jewel box glittering in the velvet darkness, a kaleidoscope of light. If the luminaire on Rittenhouse Square was not perfect (the Dorchester suffered an electrical power failure that night), it came as close to perfection as could be expected from a community of fallible humans—much like Rittenhouse Square itself.

And high above those high-rises? Could those have been the ghosts of James Harper, William Divine, Henry Cohen, Elizabeth Martin, William White, and the people of Goosetown, smiling in astonishment and delight that their Square had somehow survived intact into a new millennium (Figure 9.1)?

■ FIGURE 9.1 *Millennium celebration fireworks in the Square.*
(Photograph by Armond Scavo/Earth Light Images, © 2000.)

In real life, unlike fiction, there is no final chapter. Rittenhouse Square's survival as an oasis of urban civility depends, at it always has, on Philadelphians' willingness to support it with each new generation. As this book is written, a thirty-three-story luxury high-rise called 10 Rittenhouse Square nears completion, after years of contention, on the site of James Harper's original Walnut Street home. To mollify his community critics, the developer Hal Wheeler agreed, among other things, to preserve the facade (but not the structure) of the former Rittenhouse Club, built in 1875. The architect, Robert Stern, also planned a brick veneer for the building—an unwitting acknowledgment of Harper's brickyard, which once stood on that site. In this case, as in so many others over the preceding two centuries, Rittenhouse Square continues to be characterized by compromises that the present and future make with the past.

But it is also characterized occasionally by the sort of serendipitous solutions that occur only when large numbers of people congregate in the centers of cities. By the time the new millennium arrived, the roofs of some of the tallest buildings on the Square had become perches for families of red-tailed hawks that swooped down upon the Square's pigeons with sufficient frequency to diminish a problem that had vexed the Square for more than two centuries. Similarly, the Square's chronic dog problem largely worked itself out, apparently because a new generation of dog owners disciplined themselves to pick up after their dogs and avoid the flower beds—and took the initiative to educate their fellow dog owners as well. Yet as in any human community, each solution is offset by a new problem.

What then, should be the coda to the story of Rittenhouse Square? Let us take it from a dowager overheard there in conversation with a companion, circa 2005:

"It's not what it used to be. But then, Rittenhouse Square has never been what it used to be for very long."

Notes

CHAPTER 1

1. Pennsylvania Historical Commission, *Remember William Penn*, 78.

2. Quoted in Keels, *Forgotten Philadelphia*, 11.

3. Corcoran, *Thomas Holme, Surveyor*, 129.

4. Garvan, "Proprietary Philadelphia as Artifact," 193.

5. Ibid., 194. As the Holme plan developed, the two western squares were set a little to the west of their original locations, and the original size of eight acres for each square was reduced to six acres.

6. Tatum, *Penn's Great Town*, 19.

7. List of purchasers found among papers of William Rawle, Esq., cited in Lewis, *An Essay on Original Land Titles*, appendix, 248.

8. Thomas, *An Account of Pennsylvania*, 40.

9. Benson, *The America of 1750*, 33.

10. Quoted in Scharf and Westcott, *History of Philadelphia*, 907.

11. The last public execution on Northwest Square took place February 7, 1823, when William Gross was hanged for murder. See Scharf and Westcott, *History of Philadelphia*, 1609.

12. *Commonwealth v. Alburger*, in Wharton, "Reports of Cases," 485.

13. Lewis, *The History of an Old Philadelphia Land Title*, 137.

14. Edgar Richardson, "The Athens of America," in Weigley, *Philadelphia*, 218.

15. Quoted in Cutler and Perkins, 273–276.

16. Richardson, "The Athens of America," in Weigley, *Philadelphia*, 218.

17. Morgan, *History of Philadelphia*, 237.

18. Ibid., 33.

19. Captions of sketches in D. J. Kennedy, *Sketches of Goosetown*, at Historical Society of Pennsylvania.

20. On the east side of the Square, Nicholas Easling had a frame house and brickyard on the property owned by James Stuarts. On the west, Alexander Miller made bricks on property owned by Charles Biddle and a Dr. Edwards. See Philadelphia tax records from 1800.

21. Robert D. Crompton, *John Dunlap: Publisher of the Declaration of Independence* (pamphlet).
22. Rivinus, *The Story of Rittenhouse Square*, 10.
23. *U.S. Gazette*, April 20, 1823.
24. Clark, *The Irish in Philadelphia*, 117.

CHAPTER 2

1. Rosenberg, *The Cholera Years*, 12.
2. Diary of Joseph Sill, August 3, 1832.
3. *Christian Advocate and Journal and Zion's Herald*, July 19, 1833, quoted in *History of the Methodist Episcopal Church of the Covenant and Salem Memorial Chapel* (pamphlet).
4. These were probably *Cephalanthus*, a small tree or shrub that grows in wet low ground. Charles Cohen calls them buttonball trees.
5. Coombe, *A Fifty Years' Review of the Philadelphia Conference*, 13.
6. Quoted in DiPaolo, *My Business Was to Fight the Devil*, 70.
7. "Work of God among the Brick-makers, in Schuylkill, Philadelphia," from the *Christian Advocate and Journal and Zion's Herald*, July 19, 1833, cited in *History of the Methodist Episcopal Church of the Covenant and Salem Memorial Chapel* (pamphlet).
8. "AJR," Letters to Penn column, *The Bulletin*, September 27, 1913.
9. Flanigen, *Old Time Methodism*.
10. *Christian Advocate and Journal and Zion's Herald*, July 19, 1833, in *History of the Methodist Episcopal Church of the Covenant and Salem Memorial Chapel* (pamphlet).
11. Gillespie, *A Book of Remembrance*, 13.
12. Kilns were temporary (built with the bricks themselves) or permanent. Kilns were partially closed and fired at "slow burn," 250–350°F, to steam off the water. Then the kiln was sealed and the heat raised to a "red heat" (about 1,800°F) for several days. The burning was supervised for five days and nights. Each firing required one acre of wood. Then the kiln was cooled for several days and the bricks were sorted. See Martin, "19th Century Brickmaking," 31.
13. Flanigen, *Old Time Methodism*.
14. Ibid.
15. *The Cholera Record* recorded cases and addresses daily.
16. Ibid.
17. Flanigen, *Old Time Methodism*.
18. Burke, Sperr, and McCauley, *Historic Rittenhouse*, 11.
19. Western Methodist Church records, St. George United Methodist Church Archives.
20. *Lions of Philadelphia* (pamphlet, 1839), 35.
21. See Watson, *Watson Annuals*, 1857, 232–233, for a description.

22. David Kennedy, an artist of the time who documented much of Philadelphia, described the lots along Chestnut from Nineteenth to Twentieth streets as lower than street level because they were previously used as brickyards. Spruce Street at Twenty-first Street was graded down by six feet, making old cellar floors level with the pavement. Kennedy drawings show this odd feature.

23. Nicholas B. Wainwright, "The Age of Nicholas Biddle, 1825–1841," in Weigley, *Philadelphia*, 285. In 1831 "the boxall," a single coach driven by its owner, provided hourly service from Chestnut Street to Merchant's Coffee House on Second Street: The first omnibus line was called *Jim Crow* after the famous minstrel whose picture was painted on sides. The name was soon changed to *Cinderella*. Later coaches had names such as *William Penn, Benjamin Franklin, Stephen Girard,* and *Independence.* The coaches were a "queer" shape of a long narrow shad belly, which was replaced by a square. Other routes were established on all principal streets, some running every fifteen minutes. They offered season tickets. Scharf and Westcott, *History of Philadelphia,* 2199.

24. *City Council Ordinances,* February 13, 1834.

25. Rivinus, *The Story of Rittenhouse Square,* 10.

26. Watson, *Watson Annals,* 1829 ($629,068) to 1835 ($1,332.868) to 1841 ($3,951,121).

27. The population of the city had increased 58 percent in the 1840s and 38.3 percent in the 1850s, and a large number of the new residents were Catholic. Philadelphia was a Protestant city and the center of "militant anti-Catholicism." Elizabeth M. Geffen, "Industrial Development and Social Crisis, 1841–1854," in Weigley, *Philadelphia,* 309.

28. This vinegar factory had a curious history: It had been hauled to Nineteenth and Ann (now Manning) streets from its previous location at the Navy Yard, then located on Delaware Avenue at Federal Street.

29. This party, fearing negative economic results caused by the new immigrants, advocated repeal of the 1790 naturalization law requiring a five-year residency for voting rights. They favored a stricter twenty-one-year residency requirement to correct the "undue influence and misused privileges of the foreign population." Donaghy, *Philadelphia's Finest,* 56.

30. Quoted in Wainwright, *A Philadelphia Perspective: The Diary of Sidney George Fisher* (May 12, 1844), 165.

31. Quoted in ibid.

32. Paul Jones, "Of Men and Things," *The Bulletin,* February 5, 1959.

33. Campbell, *How Unsearchable His Ways.*

34. *A Century of Faith,* 13.

35. A new church was built in 1910 and remains at this location today. Its first pastor was the Rev. Daniel Devitt.

36. Deed Book, A.W.M. 36, p. 132. Paten of City Lots, vol. 12, p. 110. Philadelphia City Archive.

37. Haviland also designed Eastern State Penitentiary and the Walnut Street Theater, which still stand.

38. For a complete description of the house see "The Physick-Roberts House," Jeffrey Barr, 1991, at the Athenaeum of Philadelphia.

39. "Letters to Penn" column, *The Bulletin*, February 12, 1916.

40. Although a lawyer, Physick was involved in a movement to introduce a silk industry to the area, but he got caught in a silkworm scheme. In 1839 the manufacture of silk had appeared to be a "highly promising business." A social commentary of 1839 predicts, "It is highly probable, that in a few years, the agreeable spectacle will be presented, of a vast silk-growing section, immediately in our vicinity, . . . and thus, will be opened a great field for industry and wealth" (Bowen, *A History of Philadelphia*, 147). A national society was formed, and many manuals were written on the topic. Several "wealthy gentlemen" were erecting buildings for feeding worms and manufacturing silk. Philip Physick and Dr. J. Clark "are progressing rapidly," or so it seemed at the time (Bowen, *A History of Philadelphia*, 148). A later commentary explains that the silk enterprise "was made so plausible to thousands who had never had a passion for speculation that they became deeply engaged; and when it was likely to fail by its excess of tree cultivators, the deceptive and knowing ones kept up the illusion by alluring promises and prospects ahead, until the confiding and innocent were overwhelmed in ruin" (Watson, *Annals of Philadelphia,* 250). Philip Physick was one of those left in ruin, and he disappears from the history of Rittenhouse Square.

41. James Harper served two terms from 1832 to 1836 as a U.S. Congressman, was active at the Franklin Institute and Academy of Fine Arts, was a member of the Board of Guardians of the Poor, served on the Board of the Philadelphia Common Council, and was president of the Masonic Temple and vice president of the Hibernian Society.

42. Quoted in Gillespie, *A Book of Remembrance*, 13.

CHAPTER 3

1. According to the Paul Kapp Historic Structures Report, "stairway led to all four floors to roof culminating with six sided, nine feet in diameter cupola 8 ft. tall and supported by six posts. It was trimmed in Grecian revival style, 6 windows 6 × 6 lights."

2. For a complete account see Frank Willing Leach, "Historic Riots and Brawls of a Quaker City," *North American*, Philadelphia, June 27, 1915. Also Lee, *The Origin and Progress of the American Party in Politics.*

3. David Luccioni, "Fire and Be Damned," unpublished dissertation, Temple University.

4. *A Century of Faith,* 10.

5. George W. Childs led one of these units protecting St. Patrick's. Others were James McTague, Patrick Kernan, Thomas O'Brien, James Brady, and Michael Sheridan; see *A Century of Faith,* 15.

6. Quoted in Harrison, *Philadelphia Merchant: The Diary of Thomas Cope*, 438.

7. Leach, "Historic Riots and Brawls of a Quaker City."

8. Quoted in Wainwright, *A Philadelphia Perspective: The Diary of Sidney George Fisher* (May 12, 1844), 166.

9. Quoted in Harrison, *Philadelphia Merchant: The Diary of Thomas Cope*, 440.

10. Consolidation was achieved through the efforts of Eli Kirk Price (a name that will figure greatly in the history of Rittenhouse Square).

11. Cohen, *Rittenhouse Square*, 84.

12. Ibid., 100. Also see Rottenberg, *The Man Who Made Wall Street*, 49. Anthony moved on to West Philadelphia in 1856, but Francis M. Drexel remained on the south side of Rittenhouse Square until his accidental death in 1863, and his wife, Catherine, remained there until her death in 1870.

13. Scharf and Westcott, *History of Philadelphia*, 1850.

14. *The Stranger's Guide in Philadelphia*. Also Cohen, *Rittenhouse Square*, 9.

15. *The Stranger's Guide in Philadelphia*, 55. City Council records note fountains, 1853; graveling walks 1859; gas lamps, 1861; seats 1862.

16. A city of Philadelphia ordinance in 1851 allocated funds for railings at Rittenhouse, Logan, and Penn squares. Cohen, *Rittenhouse Square*, cites 1853 as the date of installation.

17. Cohen, *Rittenhouse Square*, 7.

18. In an 1871 letter to his fellow Fairmount Park commissioners, Harrison proposed an art museum in the park. He said, "If we as a nation are to keep pace with the civilization and refinement of the older states of the Christian world, we too, must have our free Art Galleries and Museums, owned by, enjoyed by, and cared for by the people" (quoted in Wainwright, "Joseph Harrison, Jr.: A Forgotten Art Collector"). He suggested placing the proposed museum very close to where it is today. Ultimately the City Council would not fund it. After his death, his wife gave paintings to the Pennsylvania Academy of the Fine Arts to form the nucleus of a collection. The paintings include some of the most well-known pieces in the collection today, such as Charles Willson Peale's *The Artist in His Museum* and Benjamin West's *Christ Rejected* and *Penn's Treaty with the Indians*. In 1912 the Charles Willson Peale 1785 portrait of Franklin and 1787 portrait of Washington were added to the collection. The George Catlin collection of Indian paintings and artifacts that Harrison purchased in 1852 for $40,000 was given to the Smithsonian Institution. This important collection filled more than a freight car when it was delivered to the Smithsonian. Ibid.

19. Cohen, *Rittenhouse Square*, 261.

20. He wrote verses ("The Iron Worker and King Soloman"), published a folio volume, won medals from the American Academy of Arts and Sciences (1871), was elected to the American Philosophical Society (1864), and belonged to other "learned societies." He died in 1874, leaving seven children. Scharf and Westcott, *History of Philadelphia*, 2259.

21. Rivinus, *The Story of Rittenhouse Square*, 16. Rivinus describes the swan as "presumably marble." The catalog of an auction sale after the death of Mrs. Harrison lists a "Vatican Swan" of "Carrara marble."

22. These town houses became known as Harrison's Row and were an early experiment in community planning. They were backed by communal gardens and stables and had fourth-floor laundries and a roof deck for drying clothes.

23. Cohen, *Rittenhouse Square,* 258.

24. Ibid., 261–262.

25. U.S. Census, 1860.

26. Cohen, *Rittenhouse Square,* 14.

27. Quoted in ibid., 16.

28. In 1879, Rogers was chairman of the committee on instruction at the Pennsylvania Academy of the Fine Arts (PAFA) and an early patron of Thomas Eakins. Fairman Rogers was immortalized by Eakins in the painting *The Fairman Rogers Four-in-Hand* (see Figure 3.9). Rogers commissioned this painting for $500, which was at the time the largest amount Eakins had received for a painting. The painting shows Rogers, his wife (Rebecca Gilpin), Mrs. Rogers's sister (Mrs. Franklin Dick) and husband, and her brother George Gilpin with wife. The painting shows the "polished red and black body of the coach" and monogrammed harnesses. This was the first time that horses in motion had been depicted accurately. Rogers had bought the evolutionary Eadweard Muybridge photo of horses in motion and gave it to PAFA. Sewel, *Thomas Eakins,* 11–80.

29. Quoted in Wolf, *Portrait of an American City,* 9. He cites Alfred Bendiner.

30. William Lejée lived on the corner of Eighteenth and Walnut in a triple lot purchased from Harper in 1849. John Grigg purchased numbers 1817 and 1823 from Harper. T. White, *Philadelphia Architecture in the Nineteenth Century,* 9.

31. Ibid.

32. Aspinwall, *A Hundred Years in His House,* 5.

33. "AJR," "Men and Things," *Ledger,* September 27, 1913.

34. Quoted in Wainwright, *A Philadelphia Perspective: The Diary of Sidney George Fisher* (February 1, 1859), 316.

35. Cohen, *Rittenhouse Square,* 7.

36. Pease, *Reminiscences from Lamplight to Satellite,* 19.

37. Thomson lived at Eighteenth and Spruce from 1858 until he died, and his widow continued living there until she died in 1912. He was followed on the Square by Thomas Scott. Alexander Cassatt, president of the Pennsylvania Railroad from 1899 until 1906, lived at 202 Nineteenth Street in 1888 (Fairman Rogers's old place).

38. Ingersoll, *Our Parents: A Family Chronicle.*

39. James Harper had sold this and the two adjacent lots in 1852 to John Worrell, and ten years later Worrell sold it to the Sturgis family.

40. Ingersoll, *Our Parents: A Family Chronicle,* 14.

41. Sara Josepha Hale, "Landscape Gardening," *Godey's Lady's Book,* September 1853, 215.

42. Ordinances of the City of Philadelphia, 1841.

43. *Godey's Lady's Book,* vol. 38, 365.

44. *Godey's Lady's Book*, vol. 27 (1843), 93.

45. George Fahnestock, unpublished diary (Historical Society of Pennsylvania). The following story comes from this diary.

46. *A Manual of Coaching*, quoted in Furness, *In Memoriam*. Also Cohen, *Rittenhouse Square,* 165.

47. Pease, *Reminiscences from Lamplight to Satellite*, 4.

48. Speirs, *The Street Railway System of Philadelphia*.

49. Many times a third "helper" horse would be added at the foot of steep hills, but usually the horsecars were drawn by two horses. A sympathetic horsecar rider wrote that the cars were pulled by "a pair of horses almost unable to pull the load—many times after paying my seven cents I felt like helping to push." *The Bulletin*, December 20, 1913. The heavy cars drawn along railways were so hard on horses that they lasted only three to five years. Rohrbeck, *Pennsylvania's Street Railways*. The horsecar rail service was the beginning of the tradition of one-way streets. The sixteen-foot "cartways" could not support double-tracked lines, so parallel streets were used for the two directions.

50. Quoted in Wainwright, *A Philadelphia Perspective: The Diary of Sidney George Fisher*, entry of September 14, 1856.

51. Rottenberg, *The Man Who Made Wall Street*, 60.

52. John Cadwalader to Charles J. Cohen, June 13, 1922. Historical Society of Pennsylvania papers. Also Taylor, *Philadelphia in the Civil War*, 356.

53. Albright, *Focus on Infinity*, 73.

54. George Washington Woodward, speech at the Great Union meeting, Independence Hall, December 18, 1860. The reference to Vaux appears in Albright, *Focus on Infinity*, 95.

55. Quoted in Aspinwall, *A Hundred Years in His House,* 12–13.

56. June 28, 1863.

57. Quoted in Allen, *Life and Letters of Phillips Brooks*, 21.

58. *Pennsylvania Inquirer*, June 29, 1863.

59. Allen, *Life and Letters of Phillips Brooks*, 453.

60. Meade, *The Life and Letters of George Gordon Meade*, 12.

CHAPTER 4

1. Thomas Penn granted land for a Jewish burial ground in 1738. Two years later the congregation Mikveh Israel was formed.

2. Cohen, *Rittenhouse Square*, 172–173.

3. Rottenberg, *The Man Who Made Wall Street*, 67–68.

4. Shackleton, *The Book of Philadelphia*, 138.

5. Fairmount Park Art Association, *Sculpture of a City*.

6. Dorothy Gondos Beers, "The Centennial City, 1865–1876," in Weigley, *Philadelphia,* 428–430.

7. Quoted in the *Bulletin,* October 13, 1957.

8. Brooke E. Vincent, "The Thomas Alexander Scott House," unpublished paper, Historical Structures Reports,1989. On file at the Athenaeum, Philadelphia.

9. *Philadelphia Telegraph,* February 24, 1913.

10. McClure, "Business Interests Demanded Peace," in *Old Time Notes,* 247.

11. *Philadelphia Scrapple,* 13.

12. McClure, "Business Interests Demanded Peace," in *Old Time Notes,* 247.

13. Fahnestock, 343.

14. McClure, "Business Interests Demanded Peace," in *Old Time Notes,* 247.

15. Quoted in Wainwright, *A Philadelphia Perspective: The Diary of Sidney George Fisher* (January 20, 1868), 536.

16. Quoted in Beers, "The Centennial City," in Weigley, *Philadelphia,* 459 (citing McClure, *Old Time Notes,* 248).

17. Cohen, *Rittenhouse Square,* 155. Mrs. Gillespie lived at 250 South Twenty-first Street.

18. For a list of committee members and their addresses, see ibid., 154–155.

19. Beers, "The Centennial City," in Weigley, *Philadelphia,* 466–470.

20. Cohen, *Rittenhouse Square,* 41–43.

21. This description was cited in a classic urban study to exemplify the vitality of a public square centered within a mixed-use environment. Jacobs, *The Death and Life of Great American Cities,* 125.

22. The DeLancey School was at this location from 1877 to 1898 and then moved to Fifteenth and Pine streets, where Peirce College is today. Episcopal Academy was at Locust and Juniper after 1849. The two schools merged in 1915 under the Episcopal name.

23. The Miss Irwins' School was at the southeast corner of Nineteenth and Spruce until 1881, when it relocated to 2011 Delancey Place. The novelist Owen Wister was the school's only male student. See Brinton, *Their Lives and Mine,* 159–160.

24. "Miss Irwin Accepts," unidentified news clip, May 1894, Campbell Collection 65-78, Pennsylvania Historical Society.

25. Brinton, *Their Lives and Mine,* 161.

26. Sarah Josepha Hale was editor of *Godey's Lady's Book* (see Chapter 3).

27. *Godey's Lady's Book,* November 1861.

28. Pease, *Reminiscences from Lamplight to Satellite,* 25.

29. Sisters of Notre Dame in Philadelphia, *100 Years of Teaching,* 1966. Also see *Center City Philadelphian,* October 1966, 40.

30. Cohen, *Rittenhouse Squaret,* 131–134.

31. O'Hara, *Heaven Was Not Enough,* 27–29.

32. Letter to Charles Cohen from Alfred Stoddard, 1922.

33. Pease, *Reminiscences from Lamplight to Satellite,* 31.

34. Pepper, *Philadelphia Lawyer,* 241.

35. Ibid., 22.

36. Pease, *Reminiscences from Lamplight to Satellite,* 31.

37. U.S. Census, 1870 and 1880.

38. Pease, *Reminiscences from Lamplight to Satellite,* 9–10.

39. Gillespie, *A Book of Remembrance.*

40. Quoted in Cohen, *Rittenhouse Square,* 31.

41. For more information see Clark, *The Irish Relations.*

42. Biddle, *A Casual Past,* 154.

43. Nathaniel Burt and Wallace E. Davies, "The Iron Age, 1876–1905." In Weigley, *Philadelphia,* 491.

44. See DuBois, *The Philadelphia Negro.*

45. Ibid., 139, 451.

46. Biddle, *A Casual Past,* 154.

47. Ibid. 154.

48. Pepper, *Philadelphia Lawyer,* 17.

49. Charles Bancroft, "A Century of Promenades," *Philadelphia Inquirer,* April 1, 1907, quoted in *Center City Philadelphian*, February 1967.

50. Rivinus, *A Full Life,* 16.

51. Rivinus, "Distaff Descent," 248.

52. Bancroft, "A Century of Promenades."

53. Morrison, *Main Line Country Houses,* xiii, xvi.

CHAPTER 5

1. Jackson, *Encyclopedia of Philadelphia,* vol. 4, 1033–1035.

2. Letter from "A Lady Subscriber," *Evening Bulletin,* February 2, 1884.

3. Cohen, *Rittenhouse Square,* 9.

4. J. Edgar Thomson (1808–1874) was the architect of the famous "horseshoe curve." He is also called the father of modern corporate management.

5. These Rittenhouse Square residents signed the petition: Mrs. J. E. Thomson, widow; Mrs. T. D. Smith, 1804 South Rittenhouse Square, widow; Charles W. Fox, forty-one years old, 1822 S. Rittenhouse Square; John H. Brown, seventy-five years old, 1822 South Rittenhouse Square,; Mrs. Joseph Harrison, widow; Thaddeus Norris; James Paul, sixty-eight years old; W. R. Lejée, seventy-two years old; Chas. Lennig, seventy-five years old; Mrs. L. F. Barry; Theodore L. Harrison; and L. L. Eyre.

6. Art Jury Report, 1941, quoting from an unidentified 1884 newspaper.

7. City Council minutes, 1884 (29 v. 3).

8. Rittenhouse Square Improvement Association, March 1913.

9. Ibid., 1913.

10. Art Jury Report, 1941.

11. Francis M. Drexel lived at 1900–1902 South Rittenhouse Square between 1852 and 1863. He moved to Rittenhouse Square in 1852, the same year as the Cohen family, before the heyday of either the Square or Drexel and Company. His son Anthony J. lived at 1816 South Rittenhouse Square until 1856. Francis M. Drexel's sons, A. J. and Francis A., however, established their compounds in West Philadelphia. A. J. Drexel's property dominated the block between Walnut and Locust streets between Thirty-eighth and Thirty-ninth streets. His own house had forty-one rooms. His three sons and his daughter lived in "imposing residences" within the compound. The family could go from house to house without using the public sidewalk. Biddle, *My Philadelphia Father,* 30.

12. In the 1890s, Sarah Drexel Fell Van Rensselaer lived on the northwest corner of Eighteenth and Walnut. A. J. Drexel, Jr., lived across from his sister on the northeast corner. On South Rittenhouse Square, Louise Drexel Morrell lived at number 1824, and her cousin Mary Johanna Lankenau lived at 1900–1902. George W. Childs Drexel lived at 231–233 South Eighteenth Street.

13. Biddle, *My Philadelphia Father* 52.

14. Cohen, *Rittenhouse Square,* 241–242.

15. Webster, *Philadelphia Preserved*, 129. The house was originally commissioned by Sarah's first husband, John Fell.

16. Ibid., 109.

17. Biddle, *My Philadelphia Father,* 20.

18. Baltzell, *Philadelphia Gentlemen*, 183.

19. Bullitt, *It's Not Done*, 7.

20. Biddle, *My Philadelphia Father*, 23.

21. James, *The American Scene*, 203. Also, Driver, *Passing Through*, 108.

22. James, *The American Scene*, 205–206.

23. Biddle, *My Philadelphia Father,* 15.

24. Summett Gawn, "The Charm of Rittenhouse Square," *Philadelphia Forum*, 1922.

25. Biddle, *My Philadelphia Father,* 48.

26. O'Hara, *Heaven Was Not Enough*, 7.

27. Elizabeth Martin's grandfather, Eli Kirk Price, was responsible for the consolidation of the city in 1854. The crown jewel of this unification was Fairmount Park, of which he made himself the first commissioner. Mrs. Martin's brother, Eli Kirk Price II, became the builder of the great art museum and Benjamin Franklin Parkway, and, like his grandfather, he was involved in all things related to Fairmount Park.

28. Rivinus, *A Full Life*, 14, 25.

29. Pease, *Reminiscences from Lamplight to Satellite*, 5.

30. *Philadelphia Scrapple,* by several anonymous Philadelphians, 82.

31. *Public Ledger*, March 14, 1913.

32. *Public Ledger*, March 15, 1913.

CHAPTER 6

1. Jackson, *Encyclopedia of Philadelphia*, vol. 2.

2. Cohen, *Rittenhouse Square*, 32.

3. *Philadelphia Record*, June 22, 1888.

4. Quoted in Repplier, *J. William White, M.D.*, 115.

5. Ibid., 2.

6. *Fifty Blooming Years, 1913–1963*. Elizabeth Martin founded the Garden Club of America and led it as president for the first seven years, during which it became a prestigious organization. During World War I, she helped organize the Emergency Aid. She chaired the Women's Committee of the Pennsylvania Division of the Council of National Defense. She held numerous statewide offices in the Republican Party. She was the first woman to address a national presidential convention.

7. Lowrie, *Strawberry Mansion*.

8. Repplier, *J. William White, M.D.,* 159.

9. Rivinus, *The Story of Rittenhouse Square*, 17.

10. The following account of this evening is from Rivinus, *The Story of Rittenhouse Square*.

11. *Rittenhouse Square Improvement Association Circular,* March 1913. At Urban Archives, Temple University Libraries.

12. The committee members were Miss E. Josephine Brazier, Mahlon Hutchinson, Mrs. Samuel Chew, Charles E. Ingersoll, Mrs. Theodore Frothingham, George McFadden, Mrs. C. C. Harrison, Richard Waln Meirs, Mrs. J. Willis Martin, G. Heide Norris, Mrs. J. K. Mitchell III, Eli Kirk Price II, Mrs. George S. Paterson, Thomas Robins, Miss Charlotte Siter, Edward B. Smith, Mrs. Charlton Yarnall, and J. William White. Rivinus, *The Story of Rittenhouse Square*, 19.

13. Repplier, *J. William White, M.D.*, 5.

14. Fund-raising circular, Wm. J. White papers, University of Pennsylvania Records Center, scrapbook 4.

15. The list of officers and directors contains names that appear multiple times in the history of Philadelphia civic affairs: Dr. White, E. B. Smith, G. Heide Norris, E. K. Price, Mrs. J. Willis Martin, Miss Charlotte Siter, Charles Ingersoll, Mahlon Hutchinson, Richard W. Meirs, Thomas Robins, Sidney W. Keith, and Theodore W. Cramp. Solicitation letter for funds for Rittenhouse

Square Improvement Association in the scrapbook of Dr. J. William White at the University of Pennsylvania archives.

16. Quoted in Jacobs, *The Death and Life of Great American Cities*, 135.

17. Bleznak, "A Brief History of a Small City Park," cites an interview with Cret's colleague John Harbeson on this matter.

18. Rivinus, "Distaff Descent."

19. *Telegraph*, February 24, 1913.

20. Cohen, *Rittenhouse Square*, 301.

21. *Bulletin*, November 7, 1924.

22. *Philadelphia Record*, 1916 (undated). Campbell Collection, Historical Society of Pennsylvania, vol. 92, 136–250.

23. *The Rittenhouse Square Flower Market Association, 1914–1934.*

24. Ibid.

25. "Peggy Shippen," *Public Ledger*, May 24, 1914.

26. Ibid.

27. "Rittenhouse Square a 'Flower Market,'" *Public Ledger*, May 21, 1914.

28. *Public Ledger*, April 29, 1915; Burt, *The Perennial Philadelphians*, 54.

CHAPTER 7

1. His "YMCA-like Bible classes . . . combined mayhem and Christianity for the young in a highly appetizing manner." Burt, *The Perennial Philadelphians*, 54.

2. *Philadelphia Inquirer*, April 29, 1915.

3. Ibid.

4. Fairmount Park Regulations, 1933, 502.

5. Rivinus, *The Story of Rittenhouse Square*, 27. Billy McLean was born in 1832.

6. Letter from John Harbeson to Theophilus White. Annenberg Collection Z95, box 562, Rare Books and Manuscript Library, University of Pennsylvania.

7. The Art Jury had approved all aspects of the 1913 square improvements: the 1912 marble mask, plans for Rittenhouse Square (1913 Art Jury submission 88), reproduction of antique vases (1914, 158), and revision of electric lighting design of post/lanterns pending (1914). Minutes, Fairmount Park Art Association, November 13, 1914.

8. Minutes, Fairmount Park Art Association, November 13, 1914.

9. Albert Laessle (1877–1954) was born in Philadelphia. He was a graduate of Spring Garden Institute, Drexel Institute, and the Pennsylvania Academy of the Fine Arts. Laessle used live animals as models for classes he taught at the academy, and presumably "Billy" was a family pet.

10. Quoted in Roberts and Roberts, *Triumph on Fairmount*, 20.

11. Minutes of Meeting, Board of Trustees, Fairmount Park Art Association, April 9, 1915.

12. Rivinus, "Distaff Descent," 204.

13. *Public Ledger,* July 30, 1919.

14. Fairmount Park Art Association, *Sculpture of a City,* 274.

15. Lloyd M. Abernethy, "Progressivism, 1905–1919," in Weigley, *Philadelphia,* 525.

16. Latham, *The Episcopal Academy,* 134.

17. Neel, *Miss Irwin's of Philadelphia,* 62.

18. Pepper, *Philadelphia Lawyer,* 17.

19. Unidentified newspaper clip, January 28, 1916.

20. In 1901, Sturgis Ingersoll saw his first automobile from the window at 1815 Walnut (Ingersoll, *Recollections at Eighty*). The Biddle family was the first on their block to have a motor-car, but automobiles were not what they are today. They had a Morse that had "an annoying habit of breaking down half a block from home and the old cry of 'Get a horse' was not music to our ears." Biddle, *My Philadelphia Father,* 57.

21. Cohen, *Rittenhouse Square,* 303.

22. The property was sold by the heirs of George McFadden after four years to pay taxes. The buyer, the Boxwood Corporation, leased it to W. W. Smith, who used it as parking. *Inquirer,* July 14, 1929, and *Bulletin,* 1930 (Urban Archives clipping, Temple University Libraries).

23. The architects were Sugarman, Hess, and Berger.

24. Author's 2001 interview with Margaret Lowery.

25. Doyle made his international reputation in the Roger Casement trial and defending Eamon de Valera. He was an adviser in drafting the constitution of the Irish Free State and Chairman of the American Committee of the League of Nations. He was on the Permanent Court of International Arbitration at The Hague. He had several Papal honors and several honorary degrees. He donated the Declaration of Independence plaque in the Capitol rotunda in 1932. He left money for the upkeep of Penn Treaty Park: $1,300 annually (*Inquirer,* July 18, 2004). He was President Harry S Truman's "right-hand man." "He and a small group of friends . . . bought" Ross Castle in the Lakes of Killarney—home of his wife's O'Donoghue family (*Bulletin,* Urban Archives, Temple University Libraries).

26. Thomas Wanamaker was associated with his father's business and was also the owner of the *North American,* a Philadelphia daily newspaper.

27. *Bulletin,* October 14, 1955.

28. Dennis Clark. "'Ramcat' and Rittenhouse Square: Related Communities," in Cutler and Gillette, *The Divided Metropolis,* 137.

29. Cohen, *Rittenhouse Square,* 191.

30. Klein, *Guidebook to Jewish Philadelphia,* 71–72; Arthur P. Dudden, "The City Embraces 'Normalcy,' 1919–1929." in Weigley, *Philadelphia,* 587. Also see Ludwig, *Beth Zion–Beth Israel 50th Anniversary: A History, 1946–1996,* 1–8.

31. Bullitt, *It's Not Done*, 300–301.

32. Quoted in Etting, *Philadelphia*, 40.

33. Quoted in Dorothy Gaiter, "A Fete in (and for) Rittenhouse Square," *New York Times,* June 23, 1984.

34. Etting, *Philadelphia* 12.

35. *Public Ledger,* January 26, 1932.

36. Toll and Gilliam, *Invisible Philadelphia*, 1103.

37. White, *The Philadelphia Art Alliance*, 34. Also *Founding the Hollywood Bowl* (pamphlet).

38. The people present were Mrs. Cornelius Stevenson; Eli Kirk Price II; "that marvelous dictator of art in Philadelphia" Henry LaBarr Jane; J. Howard Reber; Mrs. J. Sellers Bancroft; Mrs. John B. Roberts, president of the Browning Society; and Mrs. J. Norman Bell, president of the Savoy Opera Company. See White, *The Philadelphia Art Alliance*, 33.

39. Quoted in ibid., 34.

40. Ibid., 49.

41. Mrs. Otis Skinner in *Art Alliance Bulletin,* 1926, on acquisition of Wetherill House, p. 55.

42. He formed the Philadelphia Regional Planning Federation, the predecessor to the City Planning Commission (1932).

43. Schack, *Art and Argyrol*, 127.

44. Burt, *The Perennial Philadelphians*, 474.

45. Dudden, "The City Embraces 'Normalcy,'" in Weigley, *Philadelphia*, 594.

46. White, *Paul Philippe Cret: Architect and Teacher*, 38. The Anna Ingersoll to whom White refers lived at 1815 Walnut Street.

47. Leonard W. Boasberg, "Patron of Arts Keeps Her Eye on the Present," *Inquirer,* October 29, 1997.

48. *Bulletin,* June 24, 1934. Clip on file at Urban Archives, Temple University Libraries.

49. *Bulletin,* February 6, 1934. Clip on file at Urban Archives, Temple University Libraries.

50. *Bulletin,* April 1936. Clip on file at Urban Archives, Temple University Libraries.

51. Raymond C. Brecht, "An Opinion," *Bulletin,* March 3, 1974.

52. This proposal had to be approved by the Art Jury (1934 Submission 2626).

53. Rivinus, *The Story of Rittenhouse Square,* 38.

54. Klein, *Fairmount Park.*

55. According to the *Philadelphia Inquirer,* January 3, 1940, citing Radcliffe Archives, the frog was carved from a block of granite in Paris.

56. Letter, Eli Kirk Price III to John Harbeson, May 6, 1942. Paul Cret Papers, the Athenaeum of Philadelphia.

57. Letter, Paul Cret to Eli Kirk Price III, May 1, 1942. Paul Cret Papers, box 3, the Athenaeum of Philadelphia.

CHAPTER 8

1. William P. Harbeson, "Medieval Philadelphia," *Pennsylvania Magazine of History and Biography* (April 1943): 253.

2. Bobbye Burke, Center City Residents Association, *CCRA Commemorative Album,* 3.

3. *Bulletin,* August 9, 1946, and September 19, 1946.

4. *Bulletin,* September 19, 1946. Chairman: E. Walter Hudson; directors: William DuBarry, W. Clark Hanna, E. Walter Hudson, Mrs. Frederick Jost, Phil Klein, George Gordon Meade, James Alan Montgomery, Jr., William Morton West, Rabbi William H. Fineshriber, Dr. Harrison F. Flippin, C. Christopher Maris, Mrs. Belle McClain, Frank M. Murdoch, and Rev. E. Frank Salmon.

5. *Bulletin,* October 3, 1957.

6. *Bulletin,* January 3, 1950.

7. Memo to directors from Hudson, May 26, 1950; Special Board Meeting, June 8, 1950. CCRA Collection, Urban Archives, Temple University Libraries.

8. Letters, CCRA Collection, Urban Archives, Temple University Libraries.

9. Etting, *Philadelphia,* 12.

10. Rivinus, *The Story of Rittenhouse Square,* 45.

11. Alan Emlen, Letter to the Editor, *Inquirer,* May 25, 1951.

12. Unpublished Letter to the Editor of the *Inquirer,* W. Clark Hanna, May 26, 1951, CCRA Collection, Urban Archives, Temple University Libraries.

13. Letter from E. Walter Hudson to Mr. Lewis Vignola, Hon. Joseph Clark, Dr. Daniel Poling, and Mr. William Phillips, October 3, 1951, CCRA Collection, Urban Archives, Temple University Libraries.

14. Rishel, *The Henry P. McIlhenny Collection,* 115.

15. Henry P. McIlhenny papers, cited in Wikipedia.

16. Quoted in Rishel, *The Henry P. McIlhenny Collection,* 146.

17. Quoted in Frank Dougherty, "John McShain, 90, Builder," obituaries, *Daily News,* September 12, 1989. John McShain's construction projects include the Pentagon and the Jefferson Memorial. In Philadelphia he built the International Airport, Board of Education Building, U.S. Naval Hospital, and Municipal Services Building, among others.

18. *Sunday Bulletin,* January 8, 1950.

19. *Bulletin,* December 30, 1949.

20. The three houses stood at 1810, 1812, and 1814 South Rittenhouse Square. Eastern Baptist Theological Seminary vacated the property in 1942; see *Philadelphia* magazine, June 1951, 24. The school became the Palmer Theological Seminary of Eastern University in 2005.

21. *Bulletin,* January 3, 1950.

22. *Bulletin,* February 7, 1950.

23. Ibid.

24. Paul Jones, "Heyday of Rittenhouse Square Ended in 1920, Haymaking Much Earlier," *Evening Bulletin,* February 7, 1950. Urban Archives, Temple University Libraries.

25. *Bulletin,* December 30, 1949.

26. Jones, "Heyday of Rittenhouse Square Ended in 1920."

27. *Bulletin,* February 7, 1950.

28. *Bulletin,* August 15, 1951.

29. "Resident Group Approves Rittenhouse Square Project," *Bulletin,* March 29, 1955.

30. Letter to Paul M. Chalfin, Esq., from Michael Francis Doyle, June 13, 1955. Letter to Mr. Doyle from Mr. Chalfin, June 17, 1955. CCRA Collection, Urban Archives, Temple University Libraries.

31. "Rittenhouse Sq. Residents Oppose 22-Story Apartment," *Bulletin,* March 11, 1959.

32. "Truce Declared on Rittenhouse Sq.," *Center City Philadelphian,* February 1960.

33. "Webb and Knapp Gives Up Interest in Big Rittenhouse Sq. Apartment," *Center City Philadelphian,* September 1961.

34. Brookhouser, *Our Philadelphia,* 143.

35. *Bulletin,* October 13, 1948.

36. Unsigned letter (EWH) from 2100 Walnut Street to Assemblyman Cornelius J. Loftus, March 12, 1951, CCRA Collection, Urban Archives, Temple University Libraries.

37. Letter to Clark Hanna, March 21, 1951, CCRA Collection, Urban Archives, Temple University Libraries.

38. Report of the joint committee of the Center City Residents Association and the Rittenhouse Square Improvement Association, September 30, 1952, CCRA Collection, Urban Archives, Temple University Libraries.

39. October 9, 1961, CCRA meeting entitled "Pets and Parking," CCRA Collection, Urban Archives, Temple University Libraries.

40. Letter from Earl R. James to Mr. B. D. Walsh, January 12, 1957, CCRA Collection, Urban Archives, Temple University Libraries.

41. "Dogs' Best Friend—Mann," *Philadelphia Bulletin,* April 9, 1957.

42. Letter to Mr. Len Wolf, CCRA Collection, Urban Archives, Temple University Libraries.

43. Letter to Center City Residents Association, May 16, 1963, CCRA Collection, Urban Archives, Temple University Libraries.

44. "Rittenhouse Square Restrictions Contrary to Law, Says CCRA," *Center City Philadelphian,* 1963.

45. Letter to Raymond Entenmann from EWH, April 27, 1960, CCRA Collection, Urban Archives, Temple University Libraries.

46. "One Zoning Vote Kept Parking Lot off Border of Rittenhouse Square: Planners O.K.'d It," *Center City Philadelphian,* December 1964. "An Elegant New Landmark Is Slated for Rittenhouse Square," *Center City Philadelphian,* September 1961.

47. Mann continued to serve in city government as city representative, director of commerce, director of the Recreation Department, chairman of the Cultural Affairs Council, and member of the Art Commission. The Mann Music Center was named after him because of his role in building and managing the summer concert programs, which he continued to do until his death in 1987.

48. Frank Brookhouser, "Ends Era of Elegance at Rittenhouse Square," *Evening Bulletin,* October 22, 1972.

49. Etting, *Philadelphia,* 24.

50. Paul D. Davies, "The Rich and Famous Graced the Storied Barclay," *Daily News,* January 17, 2002.

51. CCRA Collection, Urban Archives, Temple University Libraries.

52. *Center City Philadelphian,* February 1967.

53. *Bulletin,* June 11, 1953.

54. *Bulletin,* September 14, 1951.

55. Jacobs, *The Death and Life of Great American Cities,* 297.

56. "Rittenhouse Square Improvement Asked," *Bulletin,* October 27, 1944.

57. Reports of the Rittenhouse Square committee, 1952 and 1953, CCRA Collection, Urban Archives, Temple University Libraries.

58. *Bulletin,* October 17, 1954.

59. Report, Rittenhouse Square committee of CCRA, October 23, 1953, CCRA Collection, Urban Archives, Temple University Libraries.

60. Letter from William Reinhardt, January 23, 1950, CCRA Collection, Urban Archives, Temple University Libraries.

61. *Bulletin,* March 14, 1954.

62. The Fairmount Park Commission had approved the same shortcut at Washington Square in 1947.

63. "Whereas, Rittenhouse Square is an important historical monument, being one of the five squares laid out in the original plan for Penn's Greene Countrie Towne; and

"whereas, Rittenhouse Square remains one of America's great landmarks that traditionally links us with the democratic growth of these United States; and

"whereas, Rittenhouse Square is one of only two open green areas in the southwest quarter of Central Philadelphia available for the recreation, relaxation and pleasure of the many thousands who live within its shadows and enjoy its classic beauties;

"now, therefore, be it resolved, that the Center City Residents' Association vehemently protests any violation of the boundaries of Rittenhouse Square and pledges the use of all means at its command to preserve Rittenhouse Square inviolate and to withstand any and all attempts of misguided persons or groups to defile it." CCRA file, Urban Archives, Temple University Libraries.

64. Quoted in Libby Schwartz, "Hippies . . . or a Lonely Crowd?" *Center City Philadelphian,* October 1967.

65. Letter to CCRA, June 9, 1968, CCRA Collection, Urban Archives, Temple University Libraries.

66. Letter to CCRA, July 14, 1968, CCRA Collection, Urban Archives, Temple University Libraries.

67. Schwartz, "Hippies."

68. Purdom, *When I Was Writing,* installment 2, available at www.philart.net/tompurdom/ wiwtwo.htm.

69. *Center City Philadelphian,* April 1963.

70. *Bulletin,* September 8, 1966.

71. *Center City Philadelphian,* October 1966, 5.

72. Letter to CCRA, July 24, 1967, CCRA Collection, Urban Archives, Temple University Libraries.

CHAPTER 9

1. With the demise of industries, the population slide continued into the seventies. Between 1970 and 1980 there would be a 13 percent drop in population in Philadelphia. Since 1950, four hundred thousand people had left the city. Stephanie G. Wolf, "The Bicentennial City, 1968–1982," in Weigley, *Philadelphia,* 707.

2. Hughes, "The Most Beautiful Front Lawn in America."

3. Wolf, "The Bicentennial City," in Weigley, *Philadelphia,* 708.

4. Fairmount Park Art Association Eighty-eighth Annual Report, 1960.

5. Marci Shatzman, "Claridge 'Boy' Leads Square Watchers," *Bulletin,* n.d., Temple University Urban Archives.

6. Among the first officers were Frank Binswanger, Margo Yannopoulos, Frederic Mann, Otto Sperr, and Bobbye Burke.

7. Edgar Williams, "In Urban Canyon, a Green Thumb," *Inquirer,* April 16, 1982.

8. Bregman, "Rittenhouse Square," 77.

9. *Philadelphia Inquirer,* June 3, 1991.

10. Quoted in Dorothy J. Gaiter, "A Fete in (and for) Rittenhouse Square," *New York Times Style,* June 23, 1984, 48.

11. Ibid.

12. Quoted in ibid.

13. A party for Young Friends was added to the evening. Between 1996 and 1999, the Friends of Rittenhouse Square contributed more than $150,000 toward the maintenance and beautification of the Square.

14. "Embracing Urban Oases the City's Parks Need All the Friends They Can Get, and, Luckily, They Have a Lot," editorial, *Inquirer*, June 3, 1991.

15. Bregman, "Rittenhouse Square," 77.

16. Donna St. George, "Center City Report Pleases Civic Leaders," *Inquirer*, April 20, 1990.

17. Susan Warner, "Sale Signs Decorate a Key Square: 5 Sites Offered on Rittenhouse," *Inquirer*, January 28, 1991. Page, "Rittenhouse Square Mansions," 15.

18. Page, "Rittenhouse Square Mansions," 15. Susan Warner, "McIlhenny Mansion Auction Set," *Inquirer*, September 11, 1990.

19. Warner, "Sale Signs Decorate a Key Square." Page, "Rittenhouse Square Mansions," 15.

20. Roxanne A. Jones, "Revival around Historic Square: One of William Penn's Original Squares Has Been Re-discovered by Modern Buyers Seeking a Certain Urban Ambience," *Inquirer*, July 25, 1993.

21. Howard Altman, "Steamed," *City Paper*, June 23–July 1, 1999.

22. Quoted in Susan Warner, "New Owner Plans Condominiums for Barclay Hotel," *Inquirer*, June 30, 1999.

23. Quoted in ibid.

24. Donohue, "The Barclay Is Back," 92.

Bibliography

A NOTE ABOUT SOURCES

The three best sources on the early history of Rittenhouse Square are *Rittenhouse Square Past and Present*, by Charles J. Cohen, who chronicled the Square's residents from the late nineteenth and early twentieth centuries; *The Story of Rittenhouse Square 1682–1951*, by Marion Willis Martin Rivinus, a small but very useful book; and *Historic Rittenhouse: A Philadelphia Neighborhood*, by Bobbye Burke, Otto Speer, and Hugh McCauley.

Valuable institutional sources include Philadelphia City Archives, Fairmount Park Archives, and City Council records, as well as records and minutes of the Art Jury, the Fairmount Park Commission, and the Fairmount Art Association. At the Urban Archives of Temple University, I read the papers and minutes of the Center City Residents Association (CCRA) and the Rittenhouse Square Flower Market. The Paul Cret papers at the Athenaeum and the University of Pennsylvania were an invaluable source for understanding the interaction of the architect and the patrons of the 1913 improvements to the Square. Other valuable institutional sources include the Philadelphia College of Physicians (a fount of information on the cholera epidemic of 1832); the archives of St. Patrick's Church; and the Methodist archives (a primary source of information about people who, though they were not deemed newsworthy in their day, were of importance in the history of the Square).

Many newspaper accounts from the 1830s through the 1900s, some undated, found in scrapbooks and archival files, were valuable in fleshing out the lives of early residents and understanding their social structure. So too were not only many diaries of the period, including those of Sidney George Fisher, Joseph Sill, George Fahnestock, and Thomas P. Cope, but also the scrapbooks of J. William White and Charles Cohen. Papers of the Ingersoll, Drexel, Lippincott, Harrison, Brinton, and Divine families provided insight into family dynamics. Land deeds and tax and insurance records, city directories and maps, the Philadelphia Blue Book, and the Philadelphia Social Registry were also useful in tracing the lives of many inhabitants of the Square.

The memoirs of Agnes Repplier, Ethel Barrymore, Constance O'Hara, Cordelia Drexel Biddle, and George W. Pepper were crucial to understanding the workings of the educational system and what it was like to grow up in the late nineteenth century. Much of my information on the late twentieth century was gleaned from newspapers, records of real estate transactions, and the personal recollections of residents.

BOOKS, ARTICLES, AND PAPERS

Albright, Raymond W. *Focus on Infinity: A Life of Phillips Brooks*. New York: Macmillan, 1961.

Allen, Alexander V. G. *Life and Letters of Phillips Brooks*. New York: E. P. Dutton, 1901.

Allen, William. Map of Philadelphia, 1838. Historical Society of Pennsylvania.

Aspinwall, Marguerite. *A Hundred Years in His House: The Story of the Church of the Holy Trinity on Rittenhouse Square Philadelphia, 1857–1957*. Philadelphia: Marguerite Aspinwall, 1956.

Bache, Richard Meade. *Life of General George Gordon Meade*. Philadelphia: Henry T. Coates, 1897.

Baltzell, E. Digby. *Philadelphia Gentlemen: The Making of a National Upper Class*. Philadelphia: University of Pennsylvania Press, 1958.

Bancroft, Charles. "A Century of Promenades." *Philadelphia Inquirer*, April 1, 1907, quoted in *Center City Philadelphia*, February 1967.

Bell, John D., and Francis Condie. *All Material Facts in the History of Epidemic Cholera*. Philadelphia, 1832.

Bendiner, Alfred. *Bendiner's Philadelphia*. New York: A. S. Barnes, 1964.

Benson, Adolph B. *The America of 1750: Peter Kalm's Travels in North America* (the English Version of 1770). New York: Eilson-Erickson, 1937.

Biddle, Cordelia Drexel. *My Philadelphia Father*. Garden City, N.Y.: Doubleday, 1955.

Biddle, Francis. *A Casual Past*. New York: Doubleday, 1961.

Bleznak, Sally. "A Brief History of a Small City Park: Rittenhouse Square." Unpublished paper, December 14, 1976.

Bowen, Daniel. *A History of Philadelphia, with a Notice of Villages, in the Vicinity*. Philadelphia: Daniel Bowen, 1839.

Bregman, Lillian. "Rittenhouse Square: The City's Back Yard Is Back.'" *Philadelphia* magazine (July 1989): 77.

Brinton, Mary Williams, *Their Lives and Mine*. Philadelphia: Mary Brinton, 1972.

Brookhouser, Frank. *Our Philadelphia*. New York: Doubleday, 1957.

Bullitt, William C. *It's Not Done*. New York: Harcourt, Brace, 1926.

Burke, Bobbye, Otto Sperr, and Hugh McCauley. *Historic Rittenhouse: A Philadelphia Neighborhood*. Philadelphia: University of Pennsylvania Press, 1985.

Burt, Nathaniel. *The Perennial Philadelphians*. Boston: Little Brown, 1963.

Campbell, William E. *How Unsearchable His Ways: One Hundred Twenty-fifth Anniversary, Saint Patrick's Church*. Philadelphia: Campbell, 1965.

A Century of Faith. Philadelphia: Parish of St. Patrick, 1939.

The Cholera Gazette. Philadelphia: Carey, Lea, and Blanchard, 1833.

Cholera Record. Scrapbook of newspaper clippings by Deborah Miles, 1832, 1839. Philadelphia: College of Physicians of Philadelphia.

Clark, Dennis. *The Irish in Philadelphia*. Philadelphia: Temple University Press, 1973.

———. *The Irish Relations: Trials of an Immigrant Tradition*. Rutherford, N.J.: Fairleigh Dickinson University Press, 1982.

Cohen, Charles J. *Rittenhouse Square: Past and Present*. Philadelphia: Charles J. Cohen, 1922.

———. Notes and scrapbooks. Historical Society of Pennsylvania.

Coombe, Pennell. *A Fifty Years' Review of the Philadelphia Conference*. Philadelphia: Craig Finley, 1883.

Corcoran, Irma. *Thomas Holme, Surveyor*. Philadelphia: American Philosophical Society, 1992.

Cutler, William Parker, and Julia Perkins. *Life Journals and Correspondence of Rev. Manasseh Cutler, L.L.D.* Cincinnati: Robert Clarke, 1888.

Cutler, William W., III, and Howard Gillette, Jr., eds. *The Divided Metropolis: Social and Spatial Dimensions of Philadelphia, 1800–1975*. Westport, Conn.: Greenwood Press, 1980.

DiPaolo, Joseph F. *My Business Was to Fight the Devil*. Arlington, Tex.: Tapestry Press, 1998.

Divine Family, 1849–1882. Real estate documents 17 items A 139. Historical Society of Pennsylvania.

Donaghy, Thomas J. *Philadelphia's Finest: A History of Education in the Catholic Archdiocese, 1692–1970*. Wynnewood, Pa.: Thomas J. Donaghy, 1972.

Donohue, Amy. "The Barclay Is Back." *Philadelphia* magazine (October 2002): 92.

Driver, Clive E., compiler. *Passing Through: Letters and Documents Written in Philadelphia by Famous Visitors*. Philadelphia: Rosenbach Museum and Library, 1982.

DuBois, W.E.B. *The Philadelphia Negro*. Philadelphia: University of Pennsylvania Press, 1899.

Etting, Gloria. *Philadelphia: The Intimate City*. New York: Viking Press, 1968.

Fahnestock, George. Unpublished diary. Historical Society of Pennsylvania.

Fairmount Park Art Association. *Sculpture of a City: Philadelphia's Treasures in Bronze and Stone*. New York: Walker Publishing, 1974.

Fifty Blooming Years, 1913–1963. New York: Garden Club of America, 1963.

Flanigen, J. R. *Old Time Methodism: Sketches of Its Early History*. Scrapbook, Historical Society of Pennsylvania.

Furness, Horace Howard. *F. R. In Memoriam*. Philadelphia: Privately printed, 1903.

Garvan, Anthony. "Proprietary Philadelphia as Artifact." In *The Historian and the City*, edited by Oscar Handlin and John E. Buchard. Cambridge, Mass.: MIT Press, 1963.

Gillespie, Mrs. E. D. *A Book of Remembrance*. Philadelphia: Lippincott, 1901.

Gillinghame, Harrold. "Some Early Brickmakers of Philadelphia. *Pennsylvania Magazine of History and Biography*, January 1929.

Harrison, Eliza Cope, ed. *Philadelphia Merchant: The Diary of Thomas P. Cope*. South Bend, Ind.: Gateway Editions, 1978.

Hexamer and Locher, surveyors. Maps of the City of Philadelphia. Vol. 3, 7th and 8th ward. Philadelphia, 1858.

Hills, John. Map of the plan of the city of Philadelphia. Historical Society of Pennsylvania, 1796.

Historical Structures Reports. Athenaeum. This is a group of unpublished student papers written for a class in documentation and archival research at the University of Pennsylvania: "The John Hare Powel Mansion," by Emily T. C. Jernigan, 1988; "The Thomas Alexander Scott House," by Brooke E. Vincent, 1989; "265 S. 19th Street," by Ellen LaPlace, 1989; "The James Harper House," by Paul Kapp, 1990; "Physick-Roberts House," by Jeffery Barr, 1991; "The Alexander Johnson Cassatt House," by Mary Hohl, 1993; "The Thomas Alexander Scott Residence, 1830–34 Rittenhouse Square," by James Toner, 1993.

Hughes, Samuel. "The Most Beautiful Front Lawn in America." *Philadelphia* magazine, November 1984.

Ingersoll, R. Sturgis. *Our Parents: A Family Chronicle*. Boyertown, Pa.: Boyertown Publishing, 1973.

———. *Recollections at Eighty*. Philadelphia: National Publishing, 1971.

Jackson, Joseph. *Encyclopedia of Philadelphia*. Harrisburg, Pa.: National Historical Association, 1933.

Jacobs, Jane. *The Death and Life of Great American Cities*. New York: Random House, 1961.

James, Henry. *The American Scene*. New York: Penguin Books, 1997.

Keels, Thomas H. *Forgotten Philadelphia: Lost Architecture of the Quaker City*. Philadelphia: Temple University Press, 2007.

Kennedy, D. J. Historical Society of Pennsylvania. Collection of articles and citations.

Klein, Esther M. *Fairmount Park, History and Guidebook*. Bryn Mawr, Pa.: Harcum Junior College Press, 1974.

———. *Guidebook to Jewish Philadelphia*. Jewish Times Institute, 1965.

Knight, Charles, Map of Philadelphia, 1838. Historical Society of Pennsylvania.

Latham, Charles, Jr. *The Episcopal Academy, 1785–1984*. Devon, Pa.: William T. Cooke Publishing, 1984.

Lednum, John. *A History of the Rise of Methodism in America*. Philadelphia: Lednum, 1859.

Lee, John Hancock. *The Origin and Progress of the American Party in Politics: Embracing a Complete History of the Philadelphia Riots in May and July 1844*. Philadelphia: Elliott and Gihon, 1855.

Lewis, John Frederick. *The History of an Old Philadelphia Land Title*. Philadelphia: Patterson and White, 1934.

Lewis, Lawrence, Jr. *An Essay on the Original Land Titles in Philadelphia*. Philadelphia: Kay and Bros., 1880.

Lowrie, Sarah Dickson. *Strawberry Mansion*. Philadelphia: Harbor Press, 1941.

Luccioni, David. "Fire and Be Damned." Unpublished dissertation, Temple University.

Martin, Henry. "19th Century Brickmaking," p. 31 in Catalogue 80, Henry Martin Brickmaking Machine Mfg. Co., Lancaster, Pa. 1915.

McCloskey, Brian. *Active and Discontinued Philadelphia Methodist Churches*. Philadelphia, 1991.

McClure, Alexander. "Business Interests Demanded Peace"; "The Streetcar in Philadelphia." *Old Time Notes*, vol. 1. Philadelphia: John C. Winston, 1905.

Meade, George Gordon. *The Life and Letters of George Gordon Meade*. Vol. 1. New York: C. Scribner's Sons, 1913.

Morais, Henry Samuel. *The Jews of Philadelphia*. Philadelphia: Levytype, 1894.

Morgan, George. *History of Philadelphia, the City of Firsts*. Philadelphia: Historical Publication Society in Philadelphia, 1926.

Morris, Cheston. *History of the Church of the Holy Trinity, 1857–1907*. 1907.

Morrison, William. *Mainline Country Houses, 1870–1930*. New York: Acanthus Press, 2004.

Myers, Albert Cook, ed. *Narratives of Early Pennsylvania, West New Jersey and Delaware, 1630–1707*. New York: C. Scribner's Sons, 1912.

Neel, Joanne Loewe. *Miss Irwin's of Philadelphia: A History of the Agnes Irwin School*. Wynnewood, Pa.: Livingston Publishing, 1969.

O'Hara, Constance. *Heaven Was Not Enough*. Philadelphia: Lippincott, 1955.

———. "The Square with a Past." Lecture of the Rittenhouse Square Branch of the Public Library of Philadelphia on the Golden Anniversary of the Art Alliance, October 1965. Special Collections, Paley Library, Temple University.

The Ordinances of the City of Philadelphia. 1798–

Page, Andrew. "Rittenhouse Square Mansions—Cheap." *Philadelphia* magazine (February 1991): 15.

Pease, Mae Townsend. *Reminiscences from Lamplight to Satellite*. Philadelphia: Dorrance, 1960.

Penniman, James Hosmer. *Philadelphia in the Early Eighteen Hundreds*. Philadelphia: St. Stephens Church, 1923.

Pennypacker, Isaac R. *George Gordon Meade*. New York: D. Appleton, 1901.

Pennsylvania Historical Commission. *Remember William Penn*. Philadelphia: Pennsylvania Historical Commission, 1944.

Pepper, George Wharton. *Philadelphia Lawyer: An Autobiography*. Philadelphia: Lippincott, 1944.

Perry, J. B. *A Full and Complete Account of the Late Awful Riots in Philadelphia: Embellished with Ten Engravings*. Philadelphia: H. Jordan; New York: Nafis and Cornish, 1858.

Philadelphia City Business and Company Partnership Directory, 1867. Philadelphia: McElroy, 1867.

Philadelphia Scrapple, by several anonymous Philadelphians. Richmond, Va.: Dietz Press, 1956.

Repplier, Agnes. *Agnes Irwin: A Biography*. Garden City, N.Y.: Doubleday, Doran, 1934.

———. *J. William White, M.D.: A Biography*. New York: Houghton Mifflin, 1919.

Rishel, Joseph J. *The Henry P. McIlhenny Collection*. Philadelphia Museum of Art, 1987.

The Rittenhouse Square Flower Market Association, 1914–1934. Urban Archives, Temple University.

Rivinus, Marion Willis Martin. "Distaff Descent." Unpublished manuscript, 1943. Historical Society of Pennsylvania.

———. *A Full Life: December 14, 1890–December 14, 1955*. Philadelphia: S. A. Wilson, 1956.

———. *The Story of Rittenhouse Square, 1682–1951*. Philadelphia: S. A. Wilson, 1950.

Roberts, George, and Mary Roberts. *Triumph on Fairmount: Fiske Kimball and the Philadelphia Museum of Art*. Philadelphia: Lippincott, 1959.

Rohrbeck, Benson W. *Pennsylvania's Street Railways*. West Chester, Pa.: Traction Publications, 1997.

Rosenberg, Charles E. *The Cholera Years: The United States in 1832, 1849, and 1866*. Chicago: University of Chicago Press, 1962.

Rottenberg, Dan. *The Man Who Made Wall Street*. Philadelphia: University of Pennsylvania Press, 2001.

Schack, William. *Art and Argyrol: The Life and Career of Dr. Albert C. Barnes*. New York: Perpetua Books, 1963.

Scharf, Thomas, and Thompson Westcott, *History of Philadelphia, 1609–1884*. Philadelphia: L. H. Everts, 1884.

Scranton, Phillip. *Proprietary Capitalism: Textile Manufacturing at Philadelphia, 1800–1885*. Wellesley, Mass.: Cambridge University Press, 1983.

Sewel, Darrel. *Thomas Eakins*. Philadelphia: Philadelphia Museum of Art, 1982.

Shackleton, Robert. *The Book of Philadelphia*. Philadelphia: Penn Publishing, 1918.

Sill, Joseph. Unpublished diary. Historical Society of Pennsylvania, 1832.

Speirs, Frederic W. *The Street Railway System of Philadelphia: Its History and Present*. Baltimore: Johns Hopkins University Press, 1897.

Stevick, Philip. *Imagining Philadelphia: Travelers' Views of the City from 1800 to the Present*. Philadelphia: University of Pennsylvania Press, 1996.

St. George United Methodist Church Archives.

Stoddard, Richard, ed. *A Century After: Picturesque Glimpses of Philadelphia and Pennsylvania*. Philadelphia: Allen Lane and Scott, 1876.

The Stranger's Guide in Philadelphia. Philadelphia: Lindsay and Blakiston, 1856.

Tatman, Sandra L., and R. W. Moss. *Biographical Dictionary of Philadelphia Architects, 1700–1930*. Boston: G. K. Hall, 1985.

Tatum, George. *Penn's Great Town: 250 Years of Philadelphia Architecture*. Philadelphia: University of Pennsylvania Press, 1961.

Taylor, Frank H. *Philadelphia in the Civil War*. Published by the City, 1913.

Thomas, Gabriel. *An Account of Pennsylvania and West New Jersey*. Reprint from the original edition of 1698. Cleveland: Burrows Brothers, 1903.

Toll, Jean Barth, and Mildred Gilliam. *Invisible Philadelphia: Community through Volunteers*. Philadelphia: Atwater Kent Museum, 1995.

The Voyage, Shipwreck, and Miraculous Preservation of Richard Castleman, Genl., with a Description of the City of Philadelphia, 4th ed. Wigan, England: Printed by William Banks, 1787. Reprint: New York: Garland Publishing, 1972.

Wainwright, Nicholas B. "Joseph Harrison, Jr.: A Forgotten Art Collector." *Antiques* 102, no. 4 (October 1972): 660–668.

———, ed. *A Philadelphia Perspective: The Diary of Sidney George Fisher, 1834–1871*. Philadelphia: Pennsylvania Historical Society, 1967.

Watson, John F. *Annals of Philadelphia, and Pennsylvania, in the Olden Time*. Vol. 1. Philadelphia: J. M. Stoddart, 1881.

———. *Watson Annuals*. Philadelphia, 1857.

Webster, Richard. *Philadelphia Preserved*. Philadelphia: Temple University Press, 1976.

Weigley, Russell, ed. *Philadelphia: A 300-Year History*. New York: W. W. Norton, 1982.

Western Methodist Church records. St. George's Methodist Church archives.

Wharton, Thomas. "Reports of Cases in the Supreme Court of Pennsylvania." Vol. 1. Philadelphia: T. Johnson Law Bookseller, 1836.

White, J. William. Papers 1871–1925. University Archives and Records Center. University of Pennsylvania.

White, Theo B. *Philadelphia Architecture in the Nineteenth Century*. Philadelphia: University of Pennsylvania Press, 1953.

———. *The Philadelphia Art Alliance: Fifty Years, 1915–1965*. Philadelphia: University of Pennsylvania Press, 1965.

———, ed. *Paul Philippe Cret: Architect and Teacher*. Philadelphia: Art Alliance Press, 1973.

Whiteman, Maxwell. *Gentlemen in Crisis: The First Century of the Union League of Philadelphia*. Philadelphia: Winchell, 1975.

Wolf, Edwin, II. *Portrait of an American City*. Harrisburg, Pa.: Stackpole Books, 1975.

Zucker, Paul. *Town and Square: From Agora to Village Green*. New York: Columbia University Press, 1959.

NEWSPAPERS

The Bulletin
Pennsylvania Gazette
Philadelphia Inquirer
Philadelphia Record
Public Ledger
The Telegraph

PERIODICALS

Center City Philadelphian
Godey's Lady's Book
Philadelphia magazine

PAMPHLETS

Christian Advocate and Journal and Zion's Herald. July 19, 1833.

Crompton, Robert D. *John Dunlap: Publisher of the Declaration of Independence.*

History of the Methodist Episcopal Church of the Covenant and Salem Memorial Chapel.

Lions of Philadelphia, 1839.

Ludwig, Charles F. *Beth Zion–Beth Israel 50th Anniversary: A History, 1946–1996.* Philadelphia (privately printed pamphlet), 1997.

Index

Nancy M. Heinzen, a resident of Rittenhouse Square, taught and served as a counselor in the Philadelphia School District. She has long been involved as a volunteer and board member in organizations dedicated to the preservation of the Square, including Friends of Rittenhouse Square, Center City Residents Association, Rittenhouse Flower Market, and Friends of Curtis Institute.